US LIBERTY SHIP
VS
GERMAN SURFACE RAIDER

The Battle of the Atlantic 1942

MARK LARDAS

OSPREY PUBLISHING
Bloomsbury Publishing Plc
Kemp House, Chawley Park, Cumnor Hill, Oxford OX2 9PH, UK
Bloomsbury Publishing Ireland Limited,
29 Earlsfort Terrace, Dublin 2, D02 AY28, Ireland
Bloomsbury Publishing Inc.
1359 Broadway, 12th Floor, New York, NY 10018, USA
E-mail: info@ospreypublishing.com
www.ospreypublishing.com

OSPREY is a trademark of Osprey Publishing Ltd

First published in Great Britain in 2026

A catalog record for this book is available from the British Library.

ISBN: PB 9781472868695; eBook 9781472868664;
ePDF 9781472868671; XML 9781472868688

26 27 28 29 30   10 9 8 7 6 5 4 3 2 1

Artwork by Édouard A. Groult
Maps by bounford.com
Index by Mark Swift
Typeset by Lumina Datamatics Ltd
Printed by Repro India Ltd.

Osprey Publishing supports the Woodland Trust, the UK's leading woodland
conservation charity.

To find out more about our authors and books visit
www.ospreypublishing.com. Here you will find extracts, author interviews,
details of forthcoming events and the option to sign up for our newsletter.

For product safety related questions contact productsafety@bloomsbury.com

Dedication
To the men of the merchant marine of the United States in World War II.
They shared the risks of the warriors, without sharing the benefits.

Title-page photograph: While guns were the primary weapons of auxiliary
cruisers, all carried torpedo tubes as well. Torpedoes were used sparingly, but
one hit generally sank a target. (Author's Collection)

CONTENTS

INTRODUCTION

The US-flagged ship steaming slowly and alone through South Atlantic waters in the morning hours of September 27, 1942, was almost new, less than six months old, having been launched on April 14. Despite this, it was not a glamorous vessel. It was a merchant freighter, and not even one of the US Maritime Commission's showcase designs, intended to win commercial supremacy for the US Merchant Marine.

SS *Stephen Hopkins* was one of the war-emergency designs that emerged from North American shipyards – in the US Maritime Commission's parlance, an EC2-S-C1 vessel. "EC2" indicated it was a war-emergency design for a dry goods cargo ship with a waterline length of 400–450ft. The single "S" indicated it was single screw and steam-powered. "C1" meant it was the US Maritime Commission's third major design of a war-emergency cargo ship between 400ft and 450ft long and the first iteration of that design. The class was called the Liberty ship.

It was unsurprising *Stephen Hopkins* used the unrevised first design. Its keel was laid on January 2, 1942, just four days after SS *Patrick Henry*, the first Liberty ship, entered service. There had been little time to update the design plans in the eight months since *Patrick Henry*'s keel was laid, and no time to learn what revisions were needed through operational experience.

The Liberty ship was a makeshift. It was a retrograde design dating to the 19th century, built for mass production. It could carry 10,000 tons of cargo in 717,600cu ft internally. *Stephen Hopkins* was one of 260 Liberty ships ordered by the US Maritime Commission in 1941. The design was copied from the British Ocean-class freighter, simplified to facilitate fast construction.

Another compromise the US Maritime Commission made was to use vertical triple-expansion (VTE) steam engines in Liberty ships instead of the steam turbines

When built, *Stephen Hopkins* was one of dozens of Liberty ships being built at the Permanente Metals Corporation Shipyard No. 2 in Richmond, California. No one thought the ship would become noteworthy. This picture of *Stephen Hopkins*, taken shortly after launch, is one of the few pictures of it in existence. (NARA)

the US Maritime Commission preferred. Ships were needed quickly, and hulls could be completed more swiftly than the steam turbines required to drive them. VTEs could be turned out quickly to bridge the gap. The price paid for this choice was a top speed of just 11.5kn. A steam turbine would have let them reach 15–18kn.

Stephen Hopkins performed satisfactorily after it entered service on May 11, 1942. The US Maritime Commission leased their new ship to the Luckenbach Steamship Company of New York, then one of the United States' largest shipping companies. Luckenbach, in turn, ran cargoes for the War Shipping Administration (WSA). *Stephen Hopkins*'s crew was as new as the ship itself, a mix of green hands and experienced mariners pulled together from whoever was available when the ship entered service. Its master, Captain Paul Buck, was a mariner with 23 years' sea experience. He previously commanded a ship for United Fruit Line.

The new ship was homeward-bound on its first voyage, having dropped cargos at ports across the Pacific, then making its way to Africa. Its last stop had been Cape Town, South Africa. Now it was steaming in ballast toward Bahia, Brazil. There, presumably it would join a convoy for the final leg home to the United States. For now, however, it was sailing independently, unescorted. Escort ships were scarce in September 1942. The South Atlantic was far from German-occupied Europe and Africa and few U-boats could reach it. In 1942 the U-boats with the range required to reach the waters in which *Stephen Hopkins* was steaming were patrolling elsewhere. There were more lucrative targets in the Caribbean and Gulf of Mexico, especially tankers carrying petroleum from the Gulf Coast and Trinidad to East Coast refineries.

The early morning of September 27 was misty and foggy. Visibility was limited, 1NM at dawn. *Stephen Hopkins* was moving at less than 8kn. It could not go faster because the light load being carried meant the ship was riding high in the water – high enough for the top of the propeller to reach above the waterline, reducing its efficiency. The limited visibility gave the deck watch 7–8 minutes to react once they spotted anything. They had to keep a sharp lookout. Fortunately, by 0800hrs the mist was beginning to lift. Visibility increased to 2NM. Then at 0850hrs, Captain Buck saw something 2NM distant that chilled his heart: two ships, peacefully motionless in the

water. They appeared to be merchantmen, similar to ones on which he had served since age 16. Regardless, experience told him something was amiss, that these were not peaceful, merchant ships.

In wartime, legitimate merchant vessels did not linger in the middle of the ocean. They had destinations to reach and enemy ships to avoid. Encountering ships stopped in the middle of the ocean indicated a problem, for either the stopped ship or the ship stumbling across them. The stopped ship either had a mechanical problem or was lurking. Two stopped ships, not showing any signs of distress, indicated a rendezvous at sea. The only ships needing that kind of rendezvous were those without ports available to them – Axis vessels. One of the two was almost certainly an auxiliary cruiser, an armed warship. Germany sent out over a half-dozen auxiliary cruisers in 1940 and 1941, disguised as ordinary merchant ships. When they encountered a potential victim, they revealed their concealed guns and demanded surrender.

Confirming the worst fears of all aboard *Stephen Hopkins*, one of the two stopped ships sent up a flag signal: "Stop At Once." Deckhouses disappeared, shutters opened and the unknown ship bristled with guns. Captain Buck was faced with two choices: surrender or fight. He could not run – a Liberty ship was too slow to outrun an auxiliary cruiser – so, he decided to fight. There were rain squalls around; perhaps he could escape into one. Regardless, he was unwilling to surrender meekly. He had the US ensign run up, ordered the crew to battle stations, and turned away from his enemy. This offered a smaller target and brought his biggest weapon, a 20-year-old 4in gun, to a position from which it could be brought to bear. *Stephen Hopkins* would likely lose this lopsided battle, but Captain Buck was determined that the German raider would know it had been in a fight.

CHRONOLOGY

1920
October — MS *Sawokla* launched.

1921
June — SS *William F. Humphrey* launched.

1936
October 7 — MS *Cairo* launched.

1938
March 16 — MS *Santa Cruz* launched.
September 1 — SS *Connecticut* launched.

1939
April — MS *Bielsko* launched.
September — Germans seize unfinished *Bielsko* in Danzig and rename it *Bonn*.
November 6 — SS *Glengarry* launched.
December — *Santa Cruz* requisitioned by the Kriegsmarine and renamed *Thor*.

1940
March 15 — Auxiliary cruiser *Thor* enters service.
April — *Glengarry* seized by Germany and renamed *Hansa*.
October 8 — MS *American Leader* launched.
December — *Bonn* renamed *Michel*; conversion to an auxiliary cruiser begins.

1941
April — Conversion of *Cairo* to an auxiliary cruiser begins. It becomes *Stier*.
September — *Michel* commissioned as a Kriegsmarine warship.
December 7 — Japan attacks USA at Pearl Harbor.
December 11 — Germany declares war on the USA.

1942
January 14 — *Thor* departs Gironde, France to begin its second cruise.
March 20 — *Michel* departs La Pallice, France on its first raiding cruise.

April 22 — *Esau* torpedoes and sinks *Connecticut*.
May 9 — *Stier* departs Royan, France on its first raiding cruise.
June 6 — *Stier* finds, fights, and sinks SS *Stanvac Calcutta*.
June 7 — *Esau* torpedoes SS *George Clymer*. HMS *Alcantara* rescues survivors the following day. *George Clymer* is abandoned.
July 16 — *Michel* sinks *William F. Humphrey*.
September 10 — *Michel* sinks *American Leader*.
September 27 — *Stier* fights and sinks SS *Stephen Hopkins*. *Stier* is so badly damaged it is scuttled after the battle.
October 9 — *Thor* completes its second cruise arriving at Yokohama, Japan.
October 14 — *Komet* sunk in the Channel.
November 29 — *Michel* sinks *Sawokla*.
November 30 — *Uckermark* (formerly *Altmark*) explodes in Yokohama Harbor, badly damaging *Thor*, which is subsequently scrapped.

1943
February 9–13 — *Togo*, while attempting to reach the French Atlantic coast to begin a raiding cruise as auxiliary cruiser *Coronel*, is forced to return to Germany.
February 13 — *Hansa* commissioned as an auxiliary cruiser.
March 1 — *Michel* arrives in Yokohama, Japan, ending its first raiding cruise.
March — The Kriegsmarine reclassifies *Hansa* as a school and target ship.
May 21 — *Michel* departs Yokohama on its second raiding cruise.
October 17 — USS *Tarpon* sinks *Michel*.

1945
May 8 — Germany surrenders.

DESIGN AND DEVELOPMENT

Throughout history, merchant vessels – privately owned ships operated for commercial gain – were armed, if only for self-defense. With the introduction of gunpowder and naval artillery, this included large-caliber guns. From the 15th through 18th centuries, merchantmen routinely carried artillery, the number and weight of the guns depending on the risk associated with the voyage. Merchantmen plying guarded waters might be unarmed, but those undertaking long voyages to remote waters were often as well-armed as the era's warships.

Rules emerged governing the behavior of private warships. In times of war, they were issued letters of marque and reprisal, permitting naval rights. Small naval warships, up to frigates, were often repurposed merchant vessels, given a heavier battery of guns, carrying crew to service the guns and stores to feed them in lieu of cargo.

During the 19th century the armed merchantman largely vanished. Technology in the form of larger artillery, steam propulsion, and metal construction caused warship and commercial design to diverge. An effective warship needed heavy guns, armor, and engines to provide high speed, all of which took up space and weight for cargo. An effective merchantman needed carrying capacity and economical operating costs. By the end of the century warships and merchant vessels evolved into two different types, distinctive in appearance and operation. Armament was the perquisite of naval ships. International treaties outlawed letters of marque, abolishing privately owned warships.

There were exceptions, however. Large passenger liners had traits desirable in warships, especially speed and volume. Although unarmed, they could function as

scouts. They were expensive to build, but some governments saw an opportunity to increase their cruiser forces during wartime. They offered construction subsidies to commercial firms operating these liners if their vessels could be converted into auxiliary cruisers in times of war. This involved strengthening their decks to carry light and medium artillery. The national navy would requisition the liners, commissioning them as auxiliary warships. From 1880 through 1918 auxiliary cruisers served as scouts, conducted blockades, and acted as commerce raiders. Some navies, including those of France, Germany, and Russia, intended to use auxiliary cruisers to hunt down enemy merchantmen in a strategy called *guerre de course* ("commerce raiding"). They specialized in it during years of war against Britain in the 18th century.

By 1914 merchant ships were largely unarmed, even in wartime. Only national warships were armed, even if originally built for commercial purposes. International prize rules had evolved governing the use of warships and commercial ships in wartime. In an encounter, the warship fired a warning shot. The merchantman was expected to stop for examination. If the merchantman was taken as a lawful prize, the warship had to ensure the merchant crew's safety before sinking the merchantman.

The advent of the submarine changed that. The submarine was a small warship that carried few torpedoes, relying on deck guns or scuttling charges to sink unarmed merchantmen. Introduced during World War I, the submarine was too small to take a captured merchant crew aboard. For submarines, prize rules meant forcing the merchant crew to take to the merchantman's boats, an action more dangerous than housing them aboard a seagoing warship.

A typical merchantman could sink a submarine through the expedient of ramming it. A cargo ship with deck guns could fight back. Countries began arming their merchantmen, generally providing the ships with a naval guard to man the guns, and a battery heavier than that of a submarine. If nothing else, arming merchantmen forced submarines to use their limited torpedoes to sink merchantmen rather than their deck guns. Armed merchantman would return in World War II.

THE GERMAN SURFACE RAIDER

Guerre de course is a strategy typically used by weaker naval powers. With its history of maintaining a small navy, Germany was one such practitioner, using it to disrupt French maritime commerce during the Franco-Prussian War (1870–71). Germany also intended to use it as part of its 19th-century war plans against France and Russia.

In the last quarter of the 19th century the Kaiserliche Marine (the Imperial German Navy of 1871–1918) subsidized construction of fast passenger liners for conversion to auxiliary cruisers. The Kaiserliche Marine was chronically short of cruisers, and auxiliary cruisers alleviated that shortage. They were intended for use as conventional cruisers, fleet scouts, or open undisguised commerce raiders. Prior to World War I, Germany's merchant marine had 13 liners listed as reserve warships, capable of being converted to Kaiserliche Marine auxiliary cruisers.

The Kaiserliche Marine was not alone in possessing ships capable of being used as auxiliary cruisers. In 1914 Britain's Royal Navy had 26, Italy 21, France nine, the United States six, and Russia and Japan four each. Pre-World War I naval annuals, including *Brassey's*, listed the vessels in their respective navy's warship tables. (RMS *Lusitania* made the list, although it was still a civilian liner and had not been converted to a warship when it was torpedoed on May 7, 1915, by U-boat *U-20* with the loss of 1,193 passengers and crew.)

When World War I broke out on July 28, 1914, Germany's potential auxiliary cruisers were scattered around the world. Five were detained in neutral ports or seized in hostile ports. Others were found to be unsuitable for use as auxiliary cruisers or used for other purposes, such as minelaying. Only eight were commissioned in the Kaiserliche Marine as auxiliary cruisers; a ninth was created by converting the Russian liner SS *Ryazan*, captured by the light cruiser *Emden* off the Korean peninsula on August 4 and taken to the port of Tsingtao in the German-leased colony of Kiautschou, China.

These conversions were uncomplicated, since all the vessels had been built with the intention of being converted into auxiliary warships. Compartments used in peacetime as secure storage areas became magazines. Guns were installed on the weather decks where the decks had been strengthened to accept them. Racks for dropping mines were added to some. The guns were all in open, single mounts. These vessels were intended to carry a main battery of 15cm guns, supplemented by secondary 10.5cm or 8.8cm guns and a scattering of smaller quick-firing guns and machine guns.

By the late 1800s, most major powers were subsidizing construction of fast ocean liners which could be converted into auxiliary cruisers in wartime. Imperial Germany was enthusiastic about them. Former liner *Kronprinz Wilhelm*, shown here in 1915, was armed and carried weapons openly. (US Naval History and Heritage Command)

When war did break out, however, these vessels ended up being armed with whatever was available, especially those in foreign ports. Two in the Atlantic put into neutral ports, where they received guns from regular Kaiserliche Marine cruisers. In Tsingtao, two auxiliary cruisers were armed by taking guns from Kaiserliche Marine warships incapable of steaming back to Germany and which would be abandoned. Except for those vessels in Germany, this first batch of auxiliary cruisers had improvised batteries.

Fitted out and fighting openly as warships, this first generation of Kaiserliche Marine auxiliary cruisers led sometimes spectacular, but always brief, careers as commerce raiders. Between August 1914 and March 1915, they sank 29 British and French merchantmen for an aggregate 105,000 GRT of shipping destroyed. Two were sunk by Royal Navy warships. The rest had been interned in neutral ports after running out of coal. The Kaiserliche Marine armed a final merchantman (the British-built *Vienna*) as a conventional auxiliary cruiser in May 1915. Commissioned as *Meteor*, it sank five ships in the White Sea before being run down by a Royal Navy cruiser squadron on August 9, 1915.

The Kaiserliche Marine's first wave of auxiliary cruisers petered out because there was no infrastructure to support them and because they were too badly outnumbered by British and French warships. The large liners were fuel hogs, especially at high speeds. There were no colliers to resupply them, and no facilities for repair if they were damaged. Furthermore, international law limited the amount of coal they could receive in neutral ports – enough to allow them to steam to the nearest friendly port at economical speeds. Running the Royal Navy's blockade to return home to Germany made this impractical.

The British and French navies also had numerous cruisers available to hunt down the Kaiserliche Marine's auxiliary cruisers. Many came from the two navies' reserve fleets, intended for commerce protection in the event of war. Most, although too elderly to participate in a fleet action, were fast enough and armed heavily enough to defeat any German auxiliary cruiser they encountered. Even had the Kaiserliche Marine a means of refueling its auxiliary cruisers, the only way they could survive was to avoid detection by Royal Navy warships – and that made the auxiliary cruisers' task of sinking enemy merchantmen problematic.

Germany rethought its commerce-raiding strategy and concluded that striking at Britain's merchant marine was its best opportunity to bring Britain down. Although U-boats showed promise as commerce raiders, they were both poorly armed and short-ranged. In 1915 at least they were limited to the North Sea and the eastern third of the North Atlantic. The Kaiserliche Marine wanted to strike British and French shipping further distant, but to do so required more auxiliary cruisers.

In August 1915 a Kaiserliche Marine lieutenant proposed a different kind of auxiliary cruiser: a disguised warship. He recommended using a ship of 4,600 GRT, which was on the high side of average for an oceangoing merchantman of the day. Instead of speed, the ship would be chosen for endurance. His proposal specified a 38,000NM range and a cruising endurance of 140 days. The ship's battery would be concealed so it could pass as a merchant vessel, and it would have the ability to carry and lay mines.

Admiralty staff liked the concept. They started a search for a suitable vessel, finally selecting *Pungo*, a fruit boat launched in May 1914. It displaced 9,800 tons, was 405ft 10in long, and had a capacity of 4,788 GRT. Top speed was 13kn and range was 8,700NM at 12kn, the speed at which it traveled carrying bananas from Cameroon to Germany during its brief prewar career. At slower speeds, its fuel consumption dropped significantly, doubling its range. After conversion at Wilhelmshaven, it carried four 15cm SK L/45 guns, one 10.5cm SK L/45 gun, two 50cm torpedo tubes, and 500 mines.

Commissioned as *Möwe* (German for "seagull") it was the prototype for all subsequent German auxiliary cruisers for the rest of World War I. Between December 1915 and March 1917 it completed two successful cruises during which it sank a total of 40

KMS *STIER*

Kriegsmarine auxiliary cruiser *Stier* began life as the motorship *Cairo*, a freighter built to service routes between Germany and the Eastern Mediterranean. It was ordered by Atlas Levant Line and launched in 1936. *Cairo* was built at Friedrich Krupp Germaniawerft in Kiel. The Kriegsmarine requisitioned *Cairo* in November 1939. It was converted to a minelayer to support Operation *Seelöwe* (*Sea Lion*), the invasion of England. Following *Sea Lion*'s cancellation, *Cairo* was chosen for conversion to an auxiliary cruiser. Conversion work started in April 1941 at Rotterdam, and

finished at Gotenhafen (now Gdynia). The Kriegsmarine designated *Stier* as *Schiff 23*; the Royal Navy labeled it Raider J. It was rechristened *Stier* ("bull") when conversion began.

Stier departed Germany in May 1942, running the Channel to reach Royan in the Gironde Estuary. It departed France for a South Atlantic cruise. Over a four-month period, *Stier* found and sank four ships – two American, two British. In its final encounter, with *Stephen Hopkins*, it was so badly damaged it was scuttled afterward.

Displacement:	11,000 tons
Tonnage:	4,778 GRT
Dimensions:	439ft 8in × 56ft 9in × 23ft 7in
Propulsion:	One seven-cylinder diesel engine, 3,700hp, one shaft
Speed:	14kn
Range:	50,000NM at 12kn
Fuel:	Diesel
Crew:	324 officers, petty officers, and sailors
Armament (1942):	Six 15cm/45 guns (6×1), two 3.7cm/30 guns (2×1), four 2cm/30 autocannons (4×1), two 53.3cm torpedo tubes (2×1)
Aircraft:	Two Arado Ar 231 floatplanes

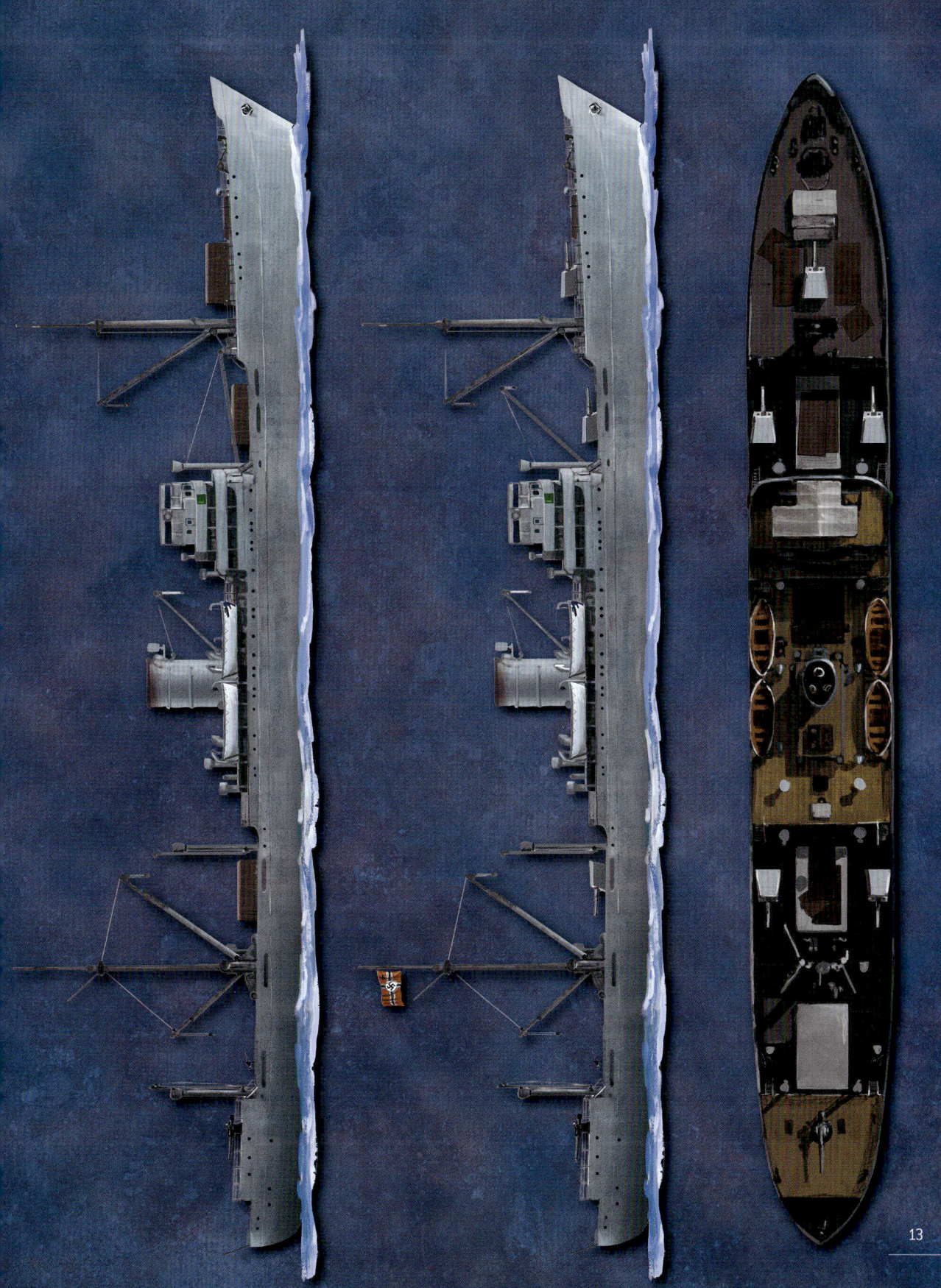

merchant ships for a total of over 180,000 GRT. It survived World War I to return to merchant service postwar. Serving as a transport in German service it was ultimately sunk by RAF Coastal Command in an air attack off the coast of Norway on April 7, 1945.

The Kaiserliche Marine converted another four merchantmen into disguised raiders in 1916. Like *Möwe*, all had concealed batteries, and depended on stealth and disguise to approach prey and evade enemy warships. Another three cruisers were converted at sea after being taken as prizes by other Kaiserliche Marine surface raiders.

While the prizes armed and commissioned as warships underwent only rudimentary conversion work (mainly in the form of adding a few guns), the conversion work done on ships dispatched from Germany was elaborate. All of the home-port conversions had main batteries of 2–7 15cm SK L/45 or L/40 guns. All but one carried mines and torpedoes. One carried a floatplane and all were elaborately disguised. In addition to concealed gun positions, they typically carried *matériel* that allowed them to change their appearance at sea, including building temporary dummy funnels and deckhouses, along with generous supplies of paint. One, the motorship *Seeadler*, had a barque sailing rig when converted. This was kept to permit the motorship to pass as a harmless sailing ship.

These converted ships attempted to pass as neutral merchant vessels, or even cargo ships flying the flags of Germany's enemies. International law allowed this deception so long as a warship dropped its false colors and raised the ensign of its proper navy before opening fire. Sometimes, as with *Möwe*, and to a lesser extent *Wolf* and *Seeadler*, these tactics yielded spectacular results. More frequently, however, the surface raiders were quickly caught.

Once at sea, the ships tied down dozens of enemy cruisers that might otherwise have been used against the Kaiserliche Marine in European waters or to support amphibious operations against Germany and its World War I allies. Combined with the toll of enemy merchant shipping, this justified the resources spent on these ships. Indeed, they returned the cost with interest.

The British-built motorship MV *Goldenfels* was typical of the freighters the Kriegsmarine planned to use as disguised auxiliary cruisers in future wars. Built in Bremen in 1937 by Bremen-Vulkan and operated by DDG Hansa from prewar, it was requisitioned by the Kriegsmarine in World War II and converted to become the auxiliary cruiser *Atlantis*.

(Author's Collection)

While the Versailles Treaty of 1919 strictly limited the size of the postwar Reichsmarine (State Navy, which replaced the Kaiserliche Marine after Kaiser's Wilhelm II's abdication on November 9, 1918), it did not restrict the size of Germany's merchant marine. Nor did it limit the number of guns 15cm and under the Reichsmarine possessed, even though it did restrict the number and displacement of vessels on which the guns were mounted. As the Reichsmarine scrapped cruisers and battleships to meet its Treaty obligations, the warships' armament went into storage.

The victors' shipyards virtually closed through much of the 1920s and early 1930s. Wartime construction of merchant ships created a postwar glut of shipping. Germany did not share in that glut, however, and surrendered much of its merchant marine that had survived the war as reparations. Except during the worst of the Great Depression, German shipyards stayed busy rebuilding Germany's merchant fleets. After the Nazis came to power in 1933, shipbuilding resumed, if only to create jobs. The result was that as the 1930s drew to a close, Germany had a generous fleet of modern merchant ships.

Before World War II started on September 1, 1939, the Kriegsmarine (War Navy) planned to use some of those vessels to supplement the fleet, as auxiliary cruisers, supply ships, and blockade runners. The selected ships shared common characteristics. They were undertaking long runs in peacetime, committed to South American, African, and Asian routes. All were capable of long ranges and could remain at sea without resupply for a minimum of 140 days, and a maximum of 352 days. All could steam at least 34,000NM at 10kn without refueling. Some had

Kormoran was one of seven disguised surface raiders sent out by the Kriegsmarine in World War II. Scuttled in the Indian Ocean after a battle with the light cruiser *HMAS Sidney* on November 19, 1941, its primary hunting ground was the southern North Atlantic Ocean. It is shown there refueling a U-boat. (Author's Collection)

a range over 60,000NM, and one could travel 84,000NM at 10kn. All were less than ten years old (most less than five years old) when the war began. All but three were diesel-powered motorships; three used steam turbines. All were oil-fueled and had a top speed of 14–18kn – a good turn of speed for a merchant vessel. They displaced 7,500–19,000 tons, with a capacity of 3,300–9,200 GRT. They were good sea boats, with high freeboard, and 6–9 watertight compartments each.

Those ships converted to auxiliary cruisers had extensive work done to them, much more so than their World War I counterparts. Quarters for prisoners were constructed and magazines were made more extensive. Underwater torpedo tubes were installed in some, as were facilities to house floatplanes and light torpedo boats. Extensive medical facilities were provided for combat casualties.

All carried a main battery of 15cm guns. Some also carried 7.5cm, 8.8cm, and 10.5cm guns and antiaircraft guns. The ships were mostly armed with guns built during World War I and subsequently held in storage. Powerful radios were installed to permit communications with Germany from the other side of the world, as was radio-jamming equipment to prevent an enemy ship under attack from transmitting a warning. A few of the converted ships were fitted with radar.

KMS *MICHEL*

KMS *Michel* was a Kriegsmarine auxiliary cruiser. It was built by the Danziger-Werft, in Danzig, and launched in April 1939 as the freighter *Bielsko*, for the Gdynia–America Line, a Polish–Danish transatlantic steamship company. Nearly completed when World War II began, it was seized as a war prize when Germany captured Danzig. Renamed *Bonn* by the Kriegsmarine, it was supposed to be converted into a hospital ship. The work dragged on, however, and in December 1940, the Kriegsmarine chose to convert it into an auxiliary cruiser. It took the guns from *Widder*, another auxiliary cruiser being converted into a repair ship after finishing a successful cruise. *Bonn* was rechristened *Michel* by its captain.

Michel proved one of the most successful German surface raiders, and the most successful of the second wave. Commissioned in September 1941, it departed Europe in January 1942. Over the course of two cruises (one leaving from Japan) it sank 18 merchant ships before being torpedoed and sunk by the US submarine *Tarpon* as it returned to Japan.

Displacement:	10,900 tons
Tonnage:	4,740 GRT
Dimensions:	433ft 1in × 55ft 1in × 24ft 3in
Propulsion:	Two MAN eight-cylinder diesel engines, 6,560hp, one shaft
Speed:	16kn
Range:	34,000NM at 10kn
Fuel:	Diesel
Crew:	377 men, 18 officers, and five prize masters
Armament (1942):	Six 15cm/45 guns (6×1), one 10.5cm/45 gun (1×1), two 3.7cm/30 guns (2×1), four 2cm/30 autocannons (4×1), 6 53.3cm torpedo tubes (2×2, 2×1), torpedo boat *LS-4*
Aircraft:	Two Arado Ar 196 floatplanes

THE US MERCHANT SHIP

By the mid-1930s the ships of the US Merchant Marine were becoming elderly. The massive shipbuilding effort the country had embarked upon during World War I saw 2,500 new merchant ships built in US shipyards between 1917 and 1922, half of which were then-modern steel-hulled steamships. The surplus resulted in fewer than 50 new merchant vessels being built over the intervening years. The Great Depression further depressed shipbuilding.

As war clouds gathered over Europe, the US government realized a new overseas war would require fleets of cargo ships and transports to support it. The United States had too small a merchant marine fleet, however. Worse, most of the ships available were overage, at least 20 years old. In response, in June 1936 the US Congress passed the Merchant Marine Act of 1936. It created the US Maritime Commission, charged with fostering a merchant shipbuilding program to build 500 modern merchant cargo ships. The Commission developed a standard set of merchant ship designs, and subsidized construction of them. The completed ships were leased to US shipping companies. They could charge lower rates, because they did not have to purchase the vessels.

When the United States finally entered World War II on December 7, 1941, the US Maritime Commission expanded its role, creating additional ship designs, under an emergency construction program. In total, this program completed 5,777 oceangoing cargo vessels for both the US Merchant Marine and the US military.

USS *Duplin* was typical of the standard US Maritime Commission dry freighter design introduced in the late 1930s. It was classified C2-S-AJ3, which means it was a dry cargo vessel, 400–450ft long (C2), steam powered with a single screw (S) using the first basic C2 design (A) and the fourth revision of that design. (Author's Collection)

The US Maritime Commission began contracting tanker designs in 1941 to fill a perceived need if the United States entered the war. To save time, they used an existing commercial design used to build the tanker SS *Mobilfuel*, shown here. Built by Bethlehem Steel, *Mobilfuel* entered service in 1939. (Author's Collection)

US MARITIME COMMISSION STANDARD DESIGNS

From 1936 until 1939 the US Maritime Commission concentrated on developing and building dry bulk cargo ships. Its goal was more than beefing up the US Merchant Marine, however. The 500 cargo ships being built (actual construction was contracted to private shipyards) were intended to serve as a reserve fleet and US Naval auxiliary warships. (Once World War II started, especially after the United States became involved, many standard design ships entered service directly as US Navy warships instead of merchant marine vessels. Several leased by merchant marine shippers were recalled and commissioned as US Navy auxiliaries.)

The US Maritime Commission started by contracting a showpiece vessel, USS *America*, a large passenger line similar to France's SS *Normandie* or Britain's RMS *Queen Mary*. Even so, *America* was intended as a troopship in the event of war. The Commission's main focus was on a set of standard break-bulk dry cargo designs to carry goods in merchant service or supplies for the military. From 1938 until 1940 the Commission concentrated on three categories of break-bulk ships: the C1, C2, and C3 standard designs.

The three categories of standard designs were differentiated by size. C1 vessels were oceangoing dry cargo vessels with a waterline length under 400ft, C2 vessels had a waterline length of 400–450ft, while C3 vessels had a waterline length of 450–500ft. Later there were C4 vessels with a waterline length of 500–550ft. (*America* was classified as a P-4: "P" for passenger ship, with "4" indicating it had a waterline length of 700–750ft.) Each design had a different intended function.

The C1 vessels were the smallest. They were to serve relatively short seagoing routes, on which speed and capacity were less important. There were several variants, the C1A and C1B being the most built. The C1A was a shelter-deck design, while the C1B was a full-scantling (transverse frame) design. The C1A had the structural weather deck one level lower than C1B, with a light superstructure, topped by a "shelter deck" above the main deck. The C1B had the scantlings (frames) run to the upper deck, with the main deck below the weather deck.

The C2 vessels, fast and fuel-efficient, were the most important. They were five-hold ships intended for transoceanic service. While the design speed was 15.5kn, many comfortably made 19kn. They had capacious holds, capable of accepting objects as large and heavy as a locomotive. While individual ships differed, costs were kept down by design and equipment standardization. Intended for commercial service, many C2 vessels were requisitioned by the US military once the US entered World War II.

The C3 vessels were larger and faster still. Also five-hold ships, whereas the C2s started at a deadweight tonnage (DWT) of 7,600 tons, the C3s were 12,500 DWT. They were designed for a top speed of 16.5kn, but frequently could add another 2–3kn to that. The C3s, too, were frequently converted to naval auxiliaries, and 22 were converted to escort carriers during or after construction.

While the US Maritime Commission emphasized dry cargo ships from 1936 through 1940, by 1940 additional tankers were deemed necessary. In 1941 the Commission added tankers to its mix of standard designs, with an initial goal of 100 to be built. As with cargo ships, the Commission developed three sets of designs – T1, T2, and T3 tankers – differentiated by their waterline length.

T1 tankers were often called "coastwise tankers" and were frequently used to carry cargos such as gasoline or liquid chemicals. T2 and T3 tankers most often carried bunker fuel or crude oil. To save time, the three tanker designs made use of plans from recently built commercial designs. All three, although intended for the US Merchant Marine, had ships requisitioned by the US Navy as fleet oilers, with some T3s converted to escort carriers.

US Maritime Commission cargo ship and tanker designs shared characteristics. All were welded, steel-hulled vessels. The cargo ships carried up to 14 5-ton cargo booms and 2–4 30-ton booms. The tankers had onboard pumps capable of

SS *STANVAC CALCUTTA*

Completed in 1941, *Stanvac Calcutta* was a T2 tanker built by Bethlehem Steel Company in Quincy, Massachusetts for Socony-Vacuum Oil Company. Stanvac, a joint venture between Socony-Vacuum and Standard Oil Company of New Jersey, served the Far East, Australia, and Eastern Africa. *Stanvac Calcutta* was added to the Stanvac fleet to move product there.

Despite being built in a US shipyard and owned by a US company, and carrying a mostly American crew, *Stanvac Calcutta* was Panamanian-registered, and flew a Panamanian flag instead of a US flag. Panama declared war on the Axis in December 1941.

Stanvac Calcutta completed its first voyage on April 25, 1942. While it was in port at Coveas, Colombia, the War Shipping Administration requisitioned it. Hastily armed, it was given a US Navy Armed Guard crew to man the guns and sent to Montevideo, Uruguay, with a load of petroleum. It departed Montevideo in ballast, to pick up a load at Caripito, Venezuela, on May 29, 1942. It encountered *Stier* 500NM off Recife, Brazil, and after a brief battle, was sunk.

Displacement:	16,400 tons
Tonnage:	10,169 GRT
Dimensions:	501ft 7in × 68ft 0in × 37ft 0in
Propulsion:	Two Westinghouse steam turbines geared to a single shaft, one screw, two water tube boilers
Speed:	15.5kn
Range:	34,000NM at 10kn
Fuel:	Bunker fuel
Crew:	42 crew, nine naval guards
Armament (1942):	One 5in/25 gun (1×1), one 4in/50 gun (1×1), four .50-caliber machine guns (4×1)

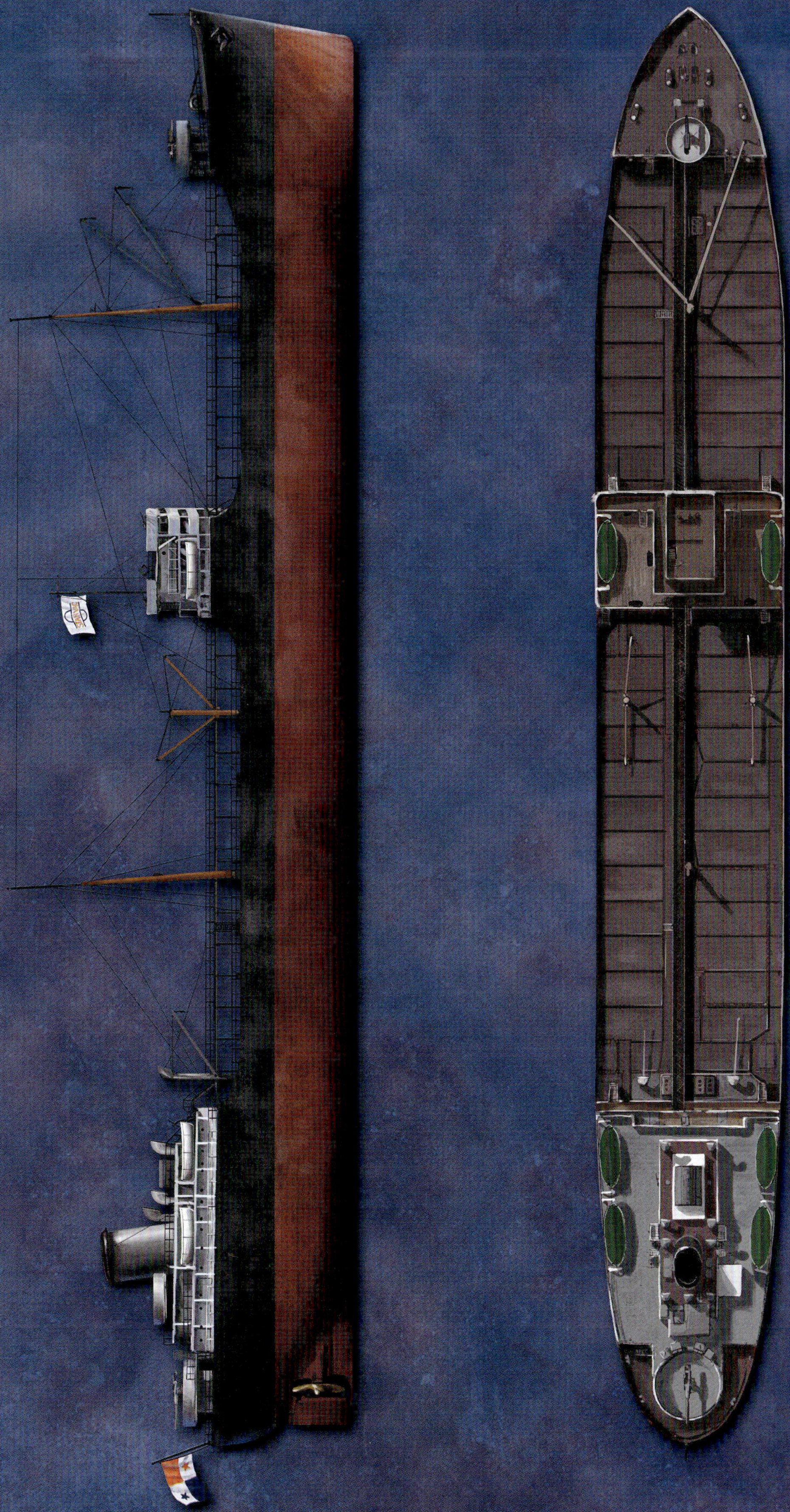

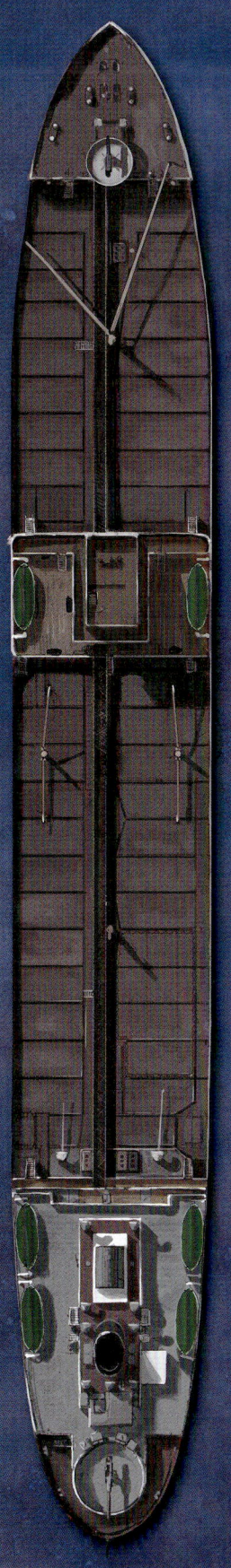

US Maritime Commission standard types				
Type	Length at waterline	DWT	Speed	Number built 1939–45
C1	up to 400ft	6,240–8,015	14kn	493
C2	400–450ft	7,640–11,300	15.5kn	328
C3	450–500ft	12,500	16.5kn	162
C4	500–550ft	15,100	17kn	81
T1	up to 450ft	2,700–5,900	12kn	113
T2	450–550ft	15,850–16,736	14kn	533
T3	500–600ft	24,830	18kn	50

loading and unloading product, and could load and unload without depending on port facilities. Crew quarters of the cargo ships and tankers were on or above the weather deck and had hot and cold running water and often air conditioning.

The US Maritime Commission favored the use of geared steam turbines, with oil-fueled boilers. This combination was the most fuel-efficient, reliable propulsion then available, but shortages of reduction gears led to the use of other propulsion systems. Some C1 and T1 vessels used marine diesels that allowed direct drive from engine to propeller. Turbo-electric and diesel-electric drives were also used. With these, the engine drove electric generators that powered electric motors driving the propellers. All these systems yielded ships capable of good speed.

In addition, the ships could be armed, their hulls being strong enough to accept a 3in to 5in gun on the bow and stern. Dual-purpose guns capable of use against both aircraft and surfaced submarines were most often mounted. The ships could also accommodate 20mm or 40mm antiaircraft guns.

WARTIME EMERGENCY DESIGNS

By 1940 it was obvious that the standard design ships, while excellent, were being produced in numbers too small for the expected wartime demand for ships. Adding tankers to the US Maritime Commission mix made things worse because tanker construction further limited the capacity available to build increased numbers of standard design freighters. In addition, standard design freighters had to compete for resources with the rapidly expanding US Navy's shipbuilding requirements as well as tankers. Reduction gears, required to transform the rotations of fast-spinning steam turbines to the much slower marine propeller speeds were in particularly short supply. Building new factories to manufacture reduction gears took years, however. Even if the gears were available, steam turbines – likewise built to extremely tight tolerances – were also scarce, as were marine diesels. The solution was two-fold: build new shipyards and build ships that did not require reduction gear, or steam turbines.

The answer lay in a British ship design being built in the United States. In 1940 Britain contracted with Todd Shipyards to build 60 Ocean-class freighters. These ships were 416ft long, had a beam of 57ft, and could carry 7,174 tons of cargo. They had a

top speed of 11kn. The design was based on the Sunderland Tramp, a ship class dating back to 1879. The major difference between the Oceans and their 19th-century ancestors was that the Oceans were oil-fired and welded rather than riveted. Both ship classes were powered by triple-expansion steam engines.

The US Maritime Commission had previously disassociated itself from this project, judging the Oceans to be too slow. Freighters were needed and needed quickly, however, and the Oceans fit that requirement. They could be built quickly, and triple-expansion engines solved the propulsion bottleneck. The Commission briefly considered using an Emergency Fleet Corporation design from World War I, the similarly sized Los Angeles class, but the design had several weaknesses, including the need to update it from riveted to welded construction. Ultimately, the Commission decided to modify the Ocean-class design for their emergency ship.

The US Maritime Commission took the Ocean-class plans and redrafted them to US standards. Water-tube boilers replaced the Scotch coal-fired boilers of the Oceans. The ships' double-bottoms were used to store fuel oil, and two deep tanks were added to the Hold 1 for water ballast. The amidships deckhouse was enlarged so the entire crew could be housed there. Steel decks and hatch covers replaced wood. Finally, a

ABOVE LEFT
The launch of SS *Zebulon B. Vance* on December 6, 1941, is shown in this picture. The last launch before Pearl Harbor brought the United States into World War II, the ceremony was more elaborate than those following. *Zebulon B. Vance* was the first Liberty ship launched by the North Carolina Shipbuilding Company. (Library of Congress)

ABOVE RIGHT
Shipyards 1–4, Richmond, California, in 1944. (Edward Cochrane, Navy Department Bureau of Ships/Wikimedia/Public Domain)

GREENFIELDS SHIPYARDS

Just as impressive as the number of new ships built for the US Maritime Commission were the number of new shipyards constructed to build them and the speed with which they were erected. At the end of 1940 there were 19 major shipyards building large ships in the United States, seven of which had been added by the US Maritime Commission since its creation on June 29, 1936. Construction of another nine shipyards with 65 building ways was approved early in 1941. These were intended just for standard design US Maritime Commission ships.

When the wartime emergency designs appeared in 1941, entirely new shipyards were needed. To build them more slips

were added to the existing shipyards, but the number would be inadequate for the desired numbers of new vessels to be built. In April 1941 the US Maritime Commission authorized construction of 11 new shipyards just to build the EC2 vessels.

The American entrepreneur and industrialist Henry J. Kaiser entered the US shipbuilding industry in 1939. By the end of 1940 his first new shipyard, at Richmond, California, entered production. In January 1942 he began a massive expansion program to build three more shipyards at Richmond, two in Portland, Oregon, and one in Vancouver, Washington. Both SS *Stephen Hopkins* and SS *George Clymer* were built in Kaiser shipyards.

The Liberty ship (this is *William Blount*) was based on an established freighter design, and used reciprocating engines that yielded a slow ship. Yet these ugly ducklings had three virtues: they could carry a large amount of cargo, they could be completed quickly, and they were cheap. (US Naval History and Heritage Command)

standardized engine design was used, with interchangeable parts, allowing any parts from one engine manufacturing plant to be used in an engine made by any other plant. The engine produced 2,500hp, and drove the Oceans at a maximum speed of 11kn.

SS *STEPHEN HOPKINS*

Stephen Hopkins was an EC2-S-C1 Liberty ship ordered by the US Maritime Commission. It was named for Stephen Hopkins, a signatory of the Declaration of Independence in 1776. Built by Kaiser, it was laid down on January 2, 1942, and launched on April 14, 1942, at the Permanente Metals Corporation Shipyard No. 2 in Richmond, California. Upon completion in May 1942, the US Maritime Commission turned the ship over to the Luckenbach Steamship Company to operate under charter for the War Shipping Administration.

On its maiden voyage it traveled to the South Pacific carrying a mixed cargo for various US Army posts there before making its way to Cape Town, South Africa. It departed Cape Town on September 19, sailing independently to Paramaribo, Dutch Guiana (now Surinam), where it was to pick up a load of bauxite. It never arrived. On September 27, 1942, just over a week out of Cape Town, it encountered the German raider *Stier* and supply ship *Tannenfels*. After a fierce engagement, in which it crippled *Stier*, *Stephen Hopkins* sank.

Displacement:	14,245 tons
Tonnage:	10,865 DWT
Dimensions:	441ft 6in × 56ft 11in × 27ft 10in
Propulsion:	One triple-expansion steam engine, one screw, two oil-fired boilers, 2,500hp
Speed:	11.5kn
Range:	20,000NM at 10kn
Fuel:	Bunker fuel
Crew:	42 crew, 15 naval guards
Armament (1942):	One 4in/50 gun (1×1), two 37mm/30 guns (1×2), two .50-caliber machine guns (2×1), two .30-caliber machine guns (2×1)

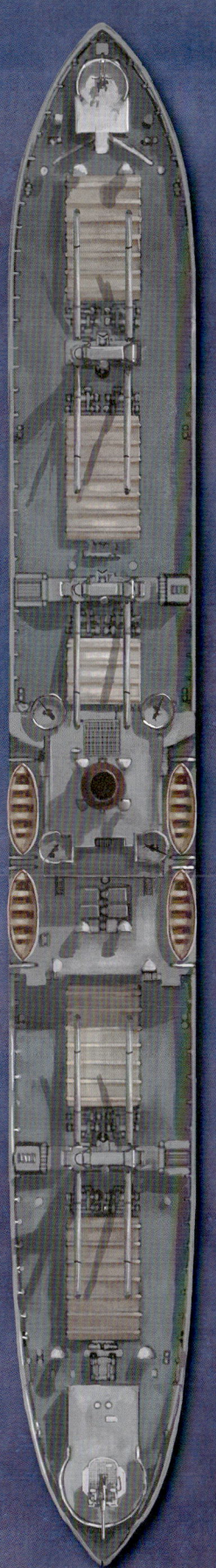

It took over six months from keel-laying to launch for the early Liberty ships. Building time quickly shrank. In 1943 construction of SS *Samuel Bowles*, shown here, was completed in just 24 days. Left, keel laying; right, launch on May 14, 1943. (Library of Congress)

The design had a gross register tonnage (GRT) of 7,176 tons, but a DWT of 10,414 tons, and displaced 14,245 tons. The difference was due to the purpose of each measurement. GRT measured the internal volume of the ship, with 100cu ft equaling one register ton. DWT was the total weight – cargo, fuel, passengers, crew, and supplies – a ship could carry. Displacement measures the total weight of the ship, including the structure. DWT and displacement were measured in long tons, 2,240lb to the ton.

The result was called the Liberty ship. The US Maritime Commission classified it as an EC2-S design: "EC" stood for Emergency Cargo, "2" meant the waterline length was between 400 and 450ft (it was 416ft with an overall length of 441.5ft), and "S" indicated it was a single-screw steamship.

What made them "emergency" ships were design factors undesirable in vessels intended for commercial profitability. Their triple-expansion engines were obsolete in 1941, and the ships were slower and less fuel-efficient than their steam-turbine counterparts. They were also optimized for fast construction rather than hydrodynamic efficiency. They had a minimum of curves, reducing the number of bends required to shape the plates to the hull form. The EC2 design had a longer parallel mid-body than similar sized C2 designs. The hull bottom was flat, curved 90 degrees where it met the sides. These design features meant the Liberty ship could be built faster than any other comparably sized vessel.

The ships were named after noteworthy Americans. The first, *Patrick Henry*, was laid down on April 30, 1941, launched on September 27, and entered service on December 30 the same year. By the time the 50th Liberty ship was started, each averaged 51 days from keel-laying to launch and one week for fitting out. It was ready to enter service in less than two months. Liberty ships formed the backbone of the US Merchant Marine's wartime shipping fleet. Before production ceased, 2,708 had been completed and commissioned.

THE STRATEGIC SITUATION

The Declaration of Paris, signed on April 16, 1856, outlawed privateering. Previously, countries could issue letters of marque and reprisal authorizing private contractors to arm ships and seize vessels owned by enemy belligerents or carrying cargos for them. Privateering often slipped into piracy, however, making it undesirable. The Declaration did not prevent national navies from incorporating merchantmen into their fleets as commissioned auxiliary warships or providing naval crews to man the guns on armed merchant vessels.

In the American Civil War (1861–65) both sides commissioned fast steam merchantmen into their fleets, armed them, and used them as warships. The Confederacy used theirs as commerce raiders, while the Union kept most of their auxiliary warships on blockade duty, freeing regular cruisers to hunt down Confederate raiders. For both, the primary objective of auxiliary warships was the enemy's merchantmen. Other countries noted this and followed suit, incorporating ships of their merchant marines into their national navies during wartime.

The trend accelerated after wireless telegraphy appeared in 1900. Fast auxiliary cruisers could now be used as scouts, permitting the regular cruisers to concentrate with the battle line. Japan used auxiliary cruisers to great effect during the Russo-Japanese War (1904–05). By World War I most naval powers incorporated auxiliary cruisers into their war plans, subsidizing construction of high-speed merchant steamships which could be converted into cruisers.

Prewar plans of navies following Alfred T. Mahan's principles of sea power largely centered on having auxiliary cruisers operate with the regular fleet, as scouts, or to support blockades. The theories of Mahan, a US Navy officer and renowned military strategist, asserted that victory depended upon three things: a powerful battle fleet to control the seas; a large merchant fleet to carry trade; and a wide network of bases for a country's naval forces and merchant marine.

Prior to World War I navies following Mahan's principles included those of the United States, Britain, Germany, and Japan. All four built large and powerful navies with which to dominate the seas. Other great powers, most notably France and Russia, could not build the requisite battle line. They opted for a strategy called *guerre de course*, or commerce raiding. This strategy relied on a large fleet of cruisers to hunt down the enemy's merchant marine while maintaining a battle line powerful enough to maintain a fleet in being. This fleet, though smaller than an opponent's, forced that opponent to keep their battle line concentrated lest the smaller enemy fleet overwhelm a portion of the larger fleet, destroying it in detail – but keeping their fleet concentrated reduced resources available to hunt down the enemy's commerce-raiding cruisers.

Guerre de course was attractive to the side with the smaller fleet. In theory, removing the enemy's merchant marine would lead to the collapse of their battle fleet, due to loss of supplies. In practice, *guerre de course* required the enemy to make mistakes for the strategy to succeed. Relying on one's enemy to fail was rarely a path to victory, however. *Guerre de course* failed France during the Napoleonic era. Germany's use of *guerre de course* during the Franco-Prussian War proved useful, but indecisive; it was one reason Kaiser Wilhelm II switched to Mahan's theories and built a large fleet prior to World War I. Prewar Germany intended for its auxiliary cruisers to operate in support of the battle fleet as scouts.

Once World War I started Germany discovered its fleet, while large, was too small to challenge Britain's Royal Navy. It ended up blockaded in its home ports, with its cruisers abroad quickly hunted down. Having failed to achieve mastery of the seas, Germany reverted to a *guerre de course* strategy, attempting to destroy the merchant marines of Britain and later its allies.

When auxiliary cruisers failed to reduce Allied shipping in World War I, Germany turned to U-boats. Initially, they proved devastatingly effective, but by 1918 Allied countermeasures completely contained them. This led the Kriegsmarine to return to surface warships for commerce raiding in prewar planning. (Library of Congress)

Starting in 1915, Germany used a combination of U-boats and disguised auxiliary cruisers to attack Britain's commerce. *Guerre de course* came close to bringing Britain to its knees, largely through Germany's use of unrestricted submarine warfare. As was typical with *guerre de course* strategies, Germany's success depended on British errors. Once implemented, effective antisubmarine warfare (ASW) measures, especially convoys, quickly ended the U-boat threat. Surface raiders proved a forlorn hope, primarily because Germany could not dispatch enough of them and no support structure existed to supply them.

Britain depended on seaborne imports to fuel its industries and feed its people. World War I demonstrated the country's vulnerability to an effective commerce-raiding campaign. Thereafter German naval war planners sought ways to cut Britain's supply lines in future wars. The Versailles Treaty strictly limited the size of Germany's fleet, however. Since Germany would now be the weaker naval power it could not blockade Britain, and had to adopt a *guerre de course* strategy.

The Kriegsmarine dismissed U-boats as commerce raiders in its prewar planning. World War I had demonstrated the U-boat's vulnerability to aircraft, and the ease with which the threat could be neutralized by convoys. (This proved to be a miscalculation in the early years of World War II, largely due to the Royal Air Force's prewar neglect of ASW aircraft and weapons. It took nearly a year for Britain to field sufficient numbers of aircraft suitable for ASW and until June 1941 to field an air-droppable depth charge.)

Instead the Kriegsmarine planned to use surface raiders. The three *Panzerschiffe* (literally "armored ships," termed "pocket battleships" by Britain) designed and started by the Reichsmarine prior to Hitler's rise to power (*Deutschland, Admiral Scheer,* and *Admiral Graf Spee*), were intended in part as long-range commerce raiders. They could operate independently over vast distances and were powerful enough to overcome any single cruiser. Since the number that could be built was treaty-limited, however, there were always too few of them to isolate Britain.

The three Deutschland-class *Panzerschiffe* (armored ships) were intended more for commerce raiding than fighting other warships. They used diesel propulsion for fuel economy yielding long range. *Admiral Scheer* conducted an Atlantic raid in 1940. (Author's Collection)

The Kriegsmarine established a network of supply ships to compensate for the lack of remote naval bases. Primarily tankers, they refueled Kriegsmarine warships at sea. *Altmark* was the most famous, used to support *Admiral Graf Spee*. *Altmark* is shown in Joessing Fjord where the British freed prisoners on it captured by *Admiral Graf Spee*. (Author's Collection)

The Kriegsmarine opted to supplement any commerce-raiding campaign with auxiliary cruisers. They were intended to be camouflaged as merchant ships, with weapons concealed until they were needed – and Germany had a pool of fast, modern, long-range cargo ships suitable for this service.

To support the *Panzerschiffe* and the auxiliary cruisers in commerce raiding, the Kriegsmarine detailed other ships in its merchant marine to serve as supply ships. They would provide the cruisers with fuel, supplies, and ammunition. The supply ships extended the range and endurance of German cruisers, allowing them to penetrate into the South Atlantic and potentially into the Indian and Pacific oceans. Since these supply ships could pass as merchant ships, they potentially could resupply in ports of sympathetic neutrals, just as any belligerent's merchant vessels could load cargo in a neutral port. An ad hoc, improvised effort in World War I would be organized and deliberate in the next war.

World War II started unexpectedly early for the Kriegsmarine, the war plan of which anticipated a 1945 start to hostilities. Few expected Britain and France to honor their guarantees to Poland, especially after they refused to support Czechoslovakia a year earlier, despite similar pledges. The Kriegsmarine was able to send *Deutschland* and *Admiral Graf Spee* on cruises before the war started in September 1939, supported by supply ships. Yet none of the auxiliary cruisers was ready. Two were dispatched in March 1940, another in May, two more in June, one in July, and a final one sailed in December 1940.

This first wave of Kriegsmarine auxiliary cruisers proved successful. Between March 1940 and November 1941, they sank or captured 99 Allied vessels (including two warships, a light cruiser, and an armed merchant cruiser). Mines laid by auxiliary cruisers sank another eight merchantmen and two trawlers. This first wave of raiders cost the Allies over 600,000 GRT of shipping. In exchange, three of the raiders sent out in 1940 were sunk.

Success depended on several factors, one of which was a porous blockade that allowed ships to escape into the North Atlantic. The Royal Navy screened the passages to the Atlantic between Greenland and Scotland largely with a collection of armed merchant cruisers and boarding ships (merchant vessels taken into Royal Navy service and armed) backed up by Royal Navy cruisers. The armed merchant

OPPOSITE

This map shows the area where the German raiders *Stier*, *Michel*, and *Thor* operated and the ships they sank in 1942.

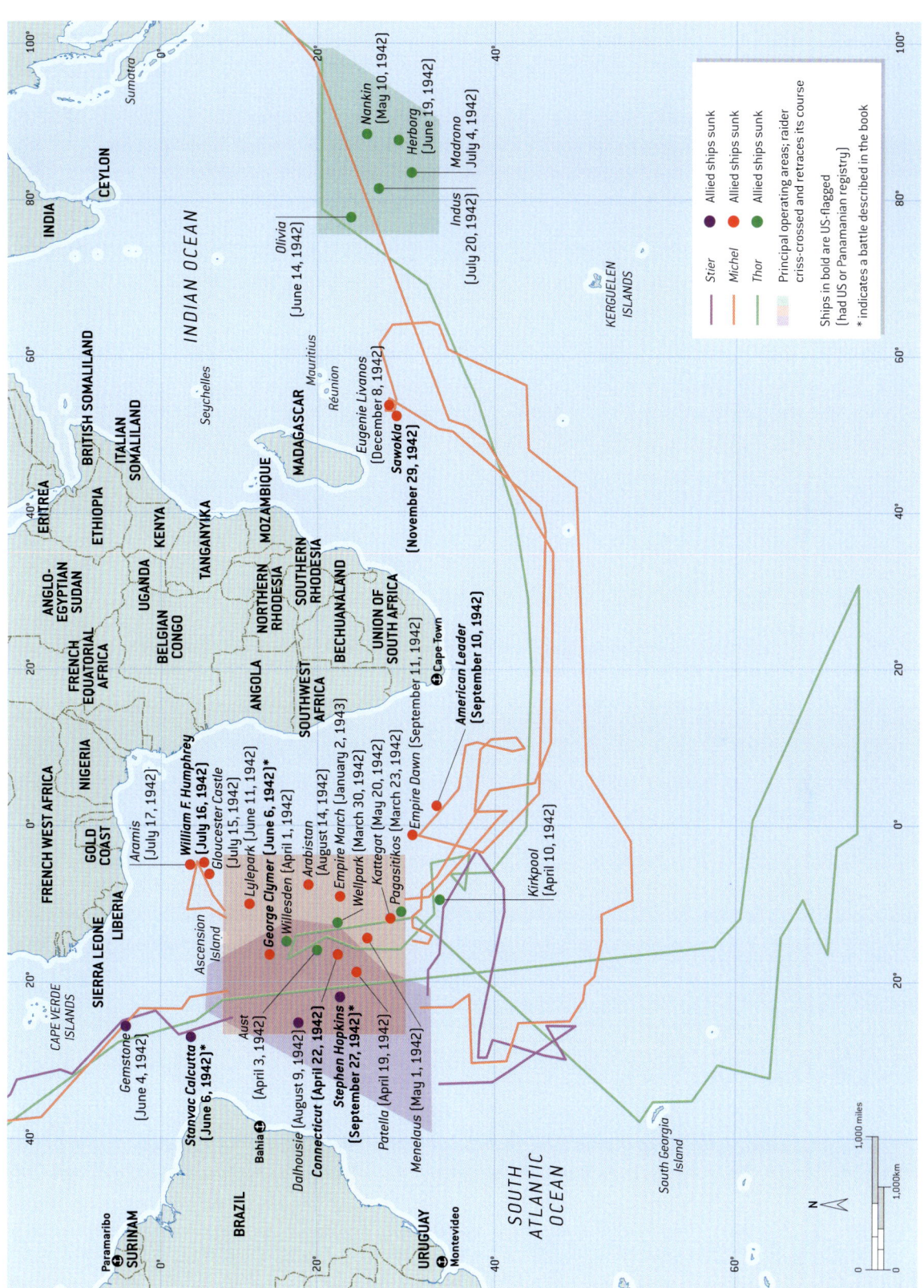

INDIA

CEYLON

INDIAN OCEAN

Sumatra

Nankin
[May 10, 1942]

Herborg
[June 19, 1942]

Madrono
[July 4, 1942]

Indus
[July 20, 1942]

Olivia
[June 14, 1942]

KERGUELEN
ISLANDS

ERITREA

ANGLO-
EGYPTIAN
SUDAN

ETHIOPIA

BRITISH SOMALILAND

ITALIAN
SOMALILAND

UGANDA

KENYA

TANGANYIKA

Seychelles

MADAGASCAR

Mauritius
Réunion

Eugenie Livanos
[December 8, 1942]

Sawokla
[November 29, 1942]

FRENCH
EQUATORIAL
AFRICA

BELGIAN
CONGO

NORTHERN
RHODESIA

ANGOLA

SOUTHERN
RHODESIA

BECHUANALAND

UNION OF
SOUTH AFRICA

Cape Town

American Leader
[September 10, 1942]

NIGERIA

FRENCH WEST AFRICA

GOLD
COAST

SOUTHWEST
AFRICA

MOZAMBIQUE

Empire Dawn [September 11, 1942]

Aramis
[July 17, 1942]

William F. Humphrey
[July 16, 1942]

Gloucester Castle
[July 15, 1942]

Lylepark [June 11, 1942]*

George Clymer [June 6, 1942]

Willesden [April 1, 1942]

Arabistan
[August 14, 1942]

Empire March [January 2, 1943]

Wellpark [March 30, 1942]

Kattegat [May 20, 1942]

Pagasitikos [March 23, 1942]

Kirkpool
[April 10, 1942]

SIERRA LEONE

LIBERIA

Ascension
Island

Aust
[April 3, 1942]

Gemstone
[June 4, 1942]

Stanvac Calcutta
[June 6, 1942]*

Bahia

Dalhousie [August 9, 1942]

Connecticut [April 22, 1942]

Stephen Hopkins
[September 27, 1942]*

Patella [April 19, 1942]

Menelaus [May 1, 1942]

CAPE VERDE
ISLANDS

BRAZIL

South Georgia
Island

SOUTH
ATLANTIC
OCEAN

URUGUAY

Montevideo

Paramaribo

SURINAM

Stier

Michel

Thor

Principal operating areas; raider
criss-crossed and retraces its course

Allied ships sunk

Allied ships sunk

Allied ships sunk

Ships in bold are US-flagged
(had US or Panamanian registry)

* indicates a battle described in the book

N

1,000 miles

1,000km

31

cruisers were a match for the German auxiliary cruisers, while the boarding ships were intended to catch unarmed blockade runners. In 1940 only the area immediately north of Scotland was patrolled by aircraft, relying exclusively on ships north of the Faroe Islands. This provided numerous opportunities to slip through the net.

Another factor was a significant neutral merchant marine. The German auxiliary cruisers depended upon disguise for survival, so they camouflaged themselves as neutral or Allied ships. The Allies knew where their merchant ships were supposed to be and (equally importantly) where they were *not* supposed to be. If a British-flagged merchantman (or one of an allied country) appeared suddenly in an unexpected location, it was a red flag that merited investigation by a Royal Navy cruiser assigned to trade protection.

Neutral shipping was not as rigorously tracked, nor could it be treated with impunity. When a Royal Navy ship ordered a British-flagged ship to stop, it did so. Neutral shipping, especially in the case of countries like Japan or the Soviet Union, could not be treated as brusquely; and in 1940 there were many neutral countries, chief among them the United States. Sweden, Spain, Portugal, and Greece also had sizable merchant fleets. Panama and Liberia, two common flags of convenience were also neutral. Some neutrals, Japan, Spain, and the Soviet Union among them, were friendly to Germany. (Soviet icebreakers plowed a path for one raider through the Arctic so it could reach the Pacific.)

As 1941 began these favorable conditions were fading. Allied maritime patrol aircraft were now present in Iceland allowing better detection of ships attempting to run the blockade in the north. More Royal Navy ships were guarding the North Atlantic approaches. While German ships gained access to the French Atlantic coast after France fell in June 1940, the Royal Navy and Royal Air Force now patrolled those waters. There were also fewer neutral countries. Norway and Denmark had been invaded by Germany in May 1940. Italy became a belligerent in June 1940. Greece entered the side of the Allies in late 1940 after Italy invaded it. On June 22, 1941, Germany invaded the Soviet Union. Then on December 7, 1941, the United States was attacked by Japan at Pearl Harbor and other sites in the Pacific and officially entered the war the next day.

Kriegsmarine U-boats had proved unexpectedly more effective as commerce raiders than had been believed prior to the war. They had limitations, however. There were still too few of them as 1942 came to an end, and they were most effective in the North Atlantic. Type VII U-boats became ineffective farther west of Greenland and Type IX U-boats had problems reaching farther south than the equator. They also carried relatively few torpedoes.

Yet the Allied merchant fleets grew during these years, despite the U-boats. Britain and the United States embarked on massive shipbuilding programs, churning out new merchantmen faster than the Kriegsmarine could sink them. Something had to be done to reduce the enemy's merchant marine. The auxiliary cruisers had been successful earlier, successful enough that the Kriegsmarine decided to send out another wave of them as surface raiders. These ships could easily reach the remote areas of the South Atlantic. The dispatch of a second wave of four auxiliary cruisers was being planned as 1941 ended and 1942 began.

TECHNICAL SPECIFICATIONS

THE KRIEGSMARINE SURFACE RAIDER

German surface raiders were drawn from a pool of merchant ships built between 1930 and 1939. All but two were German-flagged vessels before World War II. Two were suitable war prizes seized when Germany occupied Danzig and Denmark, respectively. All were structurally sound with excellent compartmentalization and had conventionally structured, longitudinally framed hulls. While intended for the merchant marine, the German-built vessels were designed with an eye toward conversion to auxiliary cruisers. The two prize vessels converted (one of which became *Michel*) possessed structural characteristics similar to the German-built vessels.

Structural modifications were required to convert the vessels to auxiliary cruisers. Decks were strengthened to accept gun mountings. Light armor was added, especially around critical areas such as the bridge. Magazines and berthing spaces for both the larger crew and expected prisoners were added, with accommodations for prisoners designed to permit their confinement. Holds were converted to serve as aircraft hangars or to accommodate and service torpedo boats. Modifications to accommodate and conceal weapons were made including cutting openings in the bulwarks to permit fields of fire, adding shutters to conceal these openings, and constructing deckhouses to cover the guns. These modifications allowed the ships to pass as ordinary merchantmen.

Concealing structure was built in such a way as to permit its quick removal. Sometimes elaborate structures were required, such as sliding deckhouses or deckhouse

Auxiliary cruisers relied on disguise for survival. Among the most effective means was making the ship appear to be a neutral merchantman. This is *Pinguin* camouflaged as the Greek-flagged *Kassos*. The reduction of neutrals throughout 1941 reduced the effectiveness of the second wave of Kriegsmarine surface raiders. (Author's Collection)

walls that collapsed. On other surface raiders the guns were disguised as lifeboats, cable drums, or locomotive fireboxes. On some surface raiders, dummy funnels, bulwarks, and deckhouses were added temporarily to change a ship's appearance and profile.

PROPULSION

Two of the three surface raiders dispatched by Germany in 1942 were diesel-powered motorships, including the two that encountered US-owned merchantmen (*Michel* and *Stier*). The third (*Thor*) used steam propulsion. In the 1930s, Germany led the world in marine diesel technology, so most of its new merchant marine vessels were propelled by low- and medium-speed diesel engines.

Michel had two MAN eight-cylinder diesel engines, each generating 3,280hp, geared to a single propeller. *Stier* had a single two-stroke seven-cylinder diesel engine, a direct drive to a single screw, generating 3,700hp. The Kriegsmarine preferred diesel propulsion for its surface raiders, and eight of the 11 deployed in World War II were powered by diesels. Diesel plants offered three distinct advantages over steam plants: simplicity, reliability, and fuel economy.

Diesel plants were mechanically simpler than steam plants. A diesel plant consisted mainly of the diesel engine itself whereas a steam plant required a boiler to produce steam, the steam engine (turbine or reciprocating), and a system to condense steam to water and clean and return feed water to the boiler. Failure or degradation of any part of the steam plant either prevented operation of the propulsion system or degraded performance significantly. Put simply, there was more that could go wrong with a steam plant. Diesels were more fault-tolerant. In extreme cases, if a cylinder failed, the ship's engineer could disconnect it and run on one less cylinder. Since the surface raiders operated on their own for extended periods, with little in the way of support or repair facilities, the less that could go wrong the better.

Diesel plants also offered greater endurance. Steam-powered *Thor* could travel 35,000NM at 10kn without refueling, but diesel-powered *Stier* could reach 43,400NM at 12kn. The few supply ships the Kriegsmarine had at sea by 1942 carried diesel, to refuel U-boats, which meant the friendly oilers diesel-powered surface raiders encountered could refuel them. Additionally, diesel-powered surface raiders could refuel U-boats at sea, whereas steam-powered surface raiders burned bunker fuel, which U-boats could not use.

Germany was a leader in the development of marine diesel engines. Simplicity, robustness, and fuel economy made them the desirable choice for auxiliary cruisers. This MAN six-cylinder marine diesel is similar to those used to power *Pinguin* and *Komet*. (Author's Collection)

WEAPONRY

The Kriegsmarine surface raiders sent out in 1942 were armed with a variety of guns, torpedoes, and mines. They carried torpedo boats and floatplanes for use both as scouts and to attack.

Guns were the surface raiders' primary armament. All three deployed in 1942 had a main battery of 15cm SK L/45 guns. Of pre-World War I origin, these guns were first used as secondary batteries on Kaiserliche Marine battleships, then reused on auxiliary cruisers and by shore batteries during World War II. They fired a 100lb projectile – deadly to merchantmen, and effective against Treaty cruisers – with a range of 19,250yd and could fire 5–7rd/min. *Michel* also carried a 10.5cm SK L/45 (salvaged off a World War I-era vessel) which fired a 38.4lb projectile with a range of 13,890yd.

HIDING GUNS

Kriegsmarine auxiliary cruisers tried to appear as harmless merchantmen. The first wave attempted to appear completely unarmed, in many cases trying to pass themselves off as neutral ships. By 1942 there were so few neutral countries that the second-wave vessels generally left their stern guns visible. When concealment became necessary, the guns had to be hidden from air search as well as observation from sea level.

The most common form of concealment was shutters, which could either drop down to conceal the guns or lift up to expose them. These were also used to conceal deck-mounted torpedo tubes. In general, shutters were used when the weapons were below the weather deck so the weather deck concealed the weapons from air search.

Guns mounted on the weather deck were concealed in a variety of ways. *Widder* hid its six 15cm SK L/45 guns using mock-ups of cable drums. Another technique was to hide them under Carley floats or house them inside fake locomotive boilers being "carried" as deck cargo. *Michel* had a sliding deckhouse for one of its six 15cm SK L/45 guns. To add verisimilitude a 2cm Flak 30 gun typical of those an armed merchantman would use for antiaircraft defense was openly mounted atop the deckhouse.

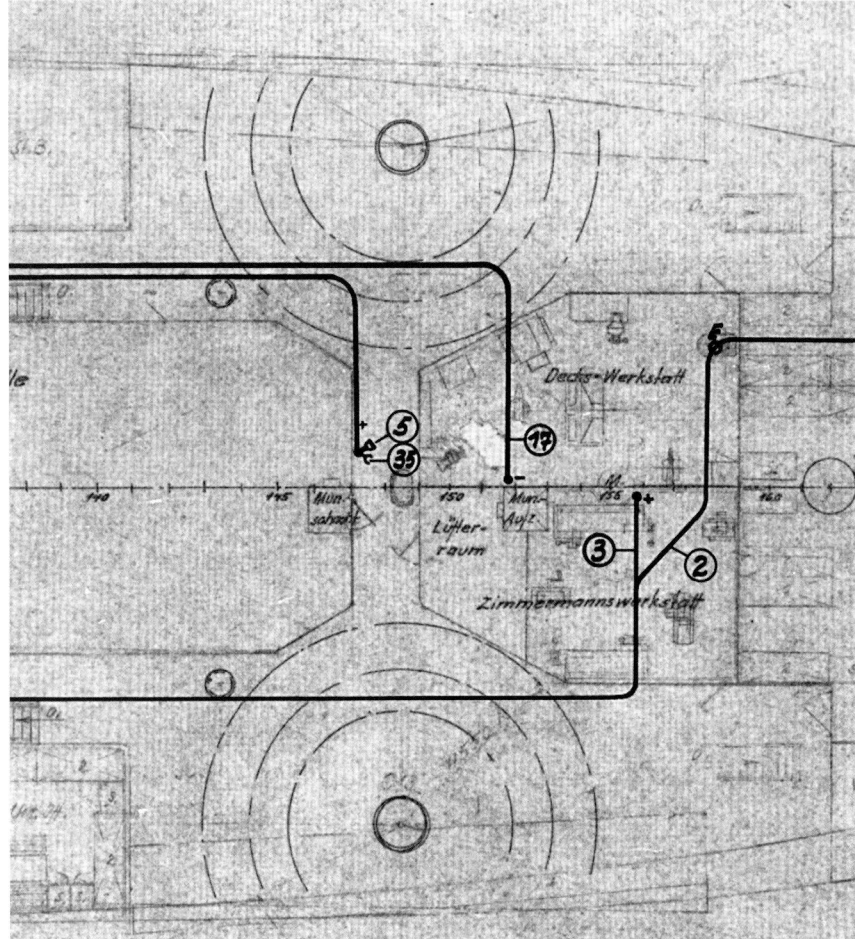

OPPOSITE

This plate shows guns carried by Kriegsmarine auxiliary cruisers. All, including *Michel* and *Stier*, carried a main battery of single-mount 15cm (5.9in) guns (**1**), typically the SK L/45 model, which predated World War I. It was the standard gun used on German light cruisers. Additionally, *Michel* carried a 10.5cm/45 (4.1in) SK C/32 (**2**). While normally used as an antiaircraft gun, *Michel* carried it to loft star shells. The Kriegsmarine auxiliary cruisers also carried a variety of light autocannons: twin-mount (**3**) and single-mount (**4**) 3.7cm/ 83 SK C/30, and single-mount 2cm/65 C/30 (**5**) guns. While they could be used as antiaircraft guns, their main purpose aboard the surface raiders was antipersonnel. They could be used to silence merchant ship gun crews, and disable their radio room and pilothouse.

For antiaircraft defense the surface raiders carried a mix of Rheinmetall 2cm/65 C/30 or C/38 autocannons and Rheinmetall 3.7cm/83 SK C/30 antiaircraft guns. The 2cm was magazine-fed and had a practical rate of fire of 120rd/min, while the 3.7cm was hand-loaded, with a maximum rate of fire of 30rd/min. Both weapons were primarily used to suppress return fire from resisting merchantmen.

The surface raiders also carried torpedo tubes. *Thor* and *Michel* had four 53.3cm tubes in twin deck mounts; *Michel* and *Stier* carried two submerged single tubes. Both the deck-mounted and submerged tubes were fixed, however, requiring the vessel to turn to aim them. The torpedoes carried were the G7a T1 (Ato), a wet-heater (or steam) design. Highly reliable, it had a range of 6,560yd at 44kn, and was armed with a 617lb Hexanite warhead.

All three surface raiders sent out in 1942 carried aircraft. *Thor* and *Michel* carried one and two Arado Ar 196 floatplanes, respectively. The Ar 196 was armed with two 7.89mm machine guns and a 2cm cannon and could carry two 50kg (110lb) bombs. It could be used to attack merchantmen or for reconnaissance. *Stier* had two Arado Ar 231 floatplanes. Because the Ar 231 was an unarmed design, it was only used for scouting. *Michel* carried a deployable motor-torpedo boat (*LS-4*, nicknamed *Esau*)

Guns concealed by movable shutters on *Atlantis*. (NARA)

armed with a 2cm autocannon and two 45cm F5b torpedoes. The F5b, Germany's aerial torpedo, had a range of 2,190yd at 40kn and was armed with a 397lb Hexanite warhead.

KRIEGSMARINE AIRCRAFT AND TORPEDO BOATS

Kriegsmarine auxiliary cruisers carried floatplanes and light torpedo boats for scouting and additional hitting power.

Stier carried two Arado Ar 231 floatplanes, while *Michel* carried two Arado Ar 196 floatplanes.

Arado Ar 196 (opposite top)	
Length:	36ft 1in
Wingspan:	40ft 8in
Armament:	2 2cm MG FF/M cannon and one 7.92mm MG 17 machine gun fixed forward firing and one 7.92mm MG 81Z machine gun flexible rear firing, two 50kg (110lb) bombs
Crew:	Two (pilot and observer)

Arado Ar 231 (opposite middle)	
Length:	25ft 7in
Wingspan:	33ft 5in
Armament:	None
Crew:	One (pilot)

LS-4 (*Esau*) (opposite below)	
Displacement:	11.5 tons
Dimensions:	41ft 0in × 11ft 4in × 2ft 11in
Propulsion:	Two Daimler-Benz MB 507 diesel engines 1,085hp
Speed:	36kn
Crew:	Seven
Armament:	One (1×1) 2cm autocannon and two 45cm (17.7in) F5b torpedoes

THE US MARITIME COMMISSION SHIP

All US Maritime Commission designs shared common design features. Steel-hulled, they were built using extensive welding, which had replaced traditional riveting. A welded hull was lighter, potentially stronger, and quicker. Riveting required plates to overlap with holes drilled through the overlap. Rivets were then driven through the holes. Hammers flattened the ends of the rivets, mushrooming the ends so they could not move. The process was time-consuming and required skilled (and strong) workmen. The overlap increased both the hull weight and the quantity of steel required to build the hull, however, and the overlap created an irregular surface, thus increasing water resistance.

Welded plates were butt-seamed, yielding a smoother surface and a lighter hull. Welding was also much faster than riveting. The weld was formed continuously, fusing the plates together. While skilled welders were required, welding required fewer workers than riveting, which required teams of two men, and more teams due to the non-continuous process in riveting.

Welding had its drawbacks, however, one of which was crack propagation. If a riveted steel plate cracked, the crack propagated the length of the plate and stopped. The ship was left with one cracked plate. If a welded ship developed a crack, additional cracks propagated past the welds. Under certain conditions this led to ships breaking

American shipbuilders used prefabricated parts to speed hull construction. The Liberty ships made the most extensive use of prefabrication. This photograph shows cranes moving a prefabricated bulwark into position on a Liberty ship under construction at Terminal Island, California. (Library of Congress)

in two as the result of a crack across the whole hull. Several Liberty ships fell apart due to crack propagation. Investigation showed the cracks were caused by notches in plates, bad steel, bad welds, and stress concentration at square corners. Improved quality control fixed steel and weld issues. A crack-arresting program added reinforcing steel to areas subject to stress concentration.

A peculiarity of Liberty ships was that they were transverse-framed, with structural frames running perpendicular to the keel. Up until the mid-1800s, most ships used transverse framing. When Isambard Kingdom Brunel built the iron-hulled SS *Great Eastern*, however, he used longitudinal framing. This permitted longer ships with greater structural strength. By the mid-20th century most ships, including US Maritime Commission designs, were longitudinally framed. Liberty ships reverted to transverse framing because it made it easier to use prefabricated hull sections. This sped production, allowing more Liberty ships to be built.

PROPULSION

For the US Merchant Marine in the mid-20th century steam was king. While other countries used marine diesels, except in special circumstances, including submarines, steam was the preferred choice for the United States' oceangoing ships. Moreover, the steam turbine was viewed as the best engine type for ships longer than 400ft.

The US Maritime Commission favored steam propulsion for American merchant shipping. Steam was reliable and flexible. Officers on the bridge could easily command a desired speed using a telegraph to tell the engine room the speed and direction the ship was to run. (US Naval History and Heritage Command)

The steam turbine used high-pressure steam to spin a turbine, a shaft with numerous small propellers attached. It imparted pure rotary motion, creating little vibration at top speed. The higher the pressure and temperature of the steam, the faster the turbine spun, and the greater the efficiency of the engine. Within limits, a bigger engine was more fuel-efficient.

The marine steam turbine's biggest drawback was that it was most efficient at rotations much higher than the speeds at which propellers turned. A geared transmission, which slowed the rotation from thousands of RPMs to 100 RPM or less, was required. The gears had to mesh perfectly and withstand high mechanical strains. This required high-tolerance machining, and specialty steels. Few facilities were capable of producing geared transmissions.

While the US Maritime Commission continued using steam turbines in its standard designs, occasionally substituting diesels in smaller vessels, it sidestepped the running gear bottleneck by equipping the Liberty ship design with a VTE steam engine. In this, steam first passed through a high-pressure cylinder. The steam exhausted from the high-pressure cylinder was used to push a medium-pressure cylinder, which exhausted into a low-pressure cylinder. From there the exhaust was captured in a condenser and returned to the boiler. The result was a reciprocating engine. Piston rods turned a crankshaft, which drove a propeller shaft. The shaft turned at the speed of the propeller, eliminating the need for a geared transmission.

A VTE engine held other advantages over steam turbines. Construction required lower tolerances and they were easier to build. Since each cylinder was an independent component, they could be manufactured at different factories and assembled as prefabricated components, permitting faster construction. The VTE engines' greatest liabilities were that they were less fuel-efficient than turbine engines, and propelled ships at slower speeds. This made them noncompetitive in a peacetime commercial service. In a war, however, commercial economics mattered less than ship availability.

WEAPONRY

American merchant vessels were unarmed until November 13, 1941, when the country's neutrality laws were amended. Thereafter the US government armed them, a process that began slowly but became standard, especially when the United States entered World War II three weeks later. Within six months all new-construction merchant ships were armed with a standard suite of weapons while fitting out. The main guns were manned by personnel from a pool drawn from the US Navy Armed Guard.

Ships typically carried a 5in/38 or 4in/50 gun aft, and a 3in/50 gun in the bow. They also carried 4–16 antiaircraft guns: .30-caliber or .50-caliber machine guns, 20mm Oerlikons, or 40mm Bofors. All were in single mounts, issued as available. In practical terms, the US Merchant Marine ships armed in 1941 and 1942 carried World War I-era 4in and 3in guns (typically landed from US Navy warships) and machine guns instead of 20mm cannon for antiaircraft protection. Or they carried whatever was at hand. (*Stephen Hopkins* carried twin 37mm cannons; *Stanvac Calcutta* carried an obsolete 3in/23 forward instead of the typical 3in/50.)

The dual-purpose 5in/38 gun – the best naval heavy antiaircraft gun of the war – was effective against surface ships, U-boats, and aircraft. It fired a 54–55.18lb projectile

43

with a range of 18,000yd at a rate of 15–22rd/min. Those on merchant ships used a simplified Mark 37 open mount.

The 4in/50 gun fired a 33–34lb round with a range of 19,600yd at a rate of 8–9rd/min. It was intended for use against surface ships, and could penetrate 3in of armor at 3,700yd. A World War I design, these guns typically came from those landed by World War I-era destroyers.

The 3in/50 was another gun dating to World War I. It was intended as an antiaircraft gun, but was effective against unarmored ships. It fired a 13lb projectile with a range of 14,000ft at a rate of 15–20rd/min.

THE COMBATANTS

The battles between Kriegsmarine surface raiders and US Merchant Marine vessels pitted two very different sets of men against each other, with only one thing in common: both were drawn from volunteers. In 1942 even the US Navy Armed Guard personnel manning the guns were volunteers. There the similarities ended.

The Kriegsmarine *Seemänner* (sailors) aboard auxiliary cruisers were picked men, capable of enduring long periods of remote service, isolated from the rest of the world, except during combat. By 1942 they were among the few members of the Kriegsmarine's surface forces taking the war to the Allies in the enemy's home waters.

Merchant marine sailors aboard merchant marine vessels of all countries, including the United States, were civilians. They were volunteers, but for them this was a job, a way to earn a living. Some were motivated to become mariners due to the romance of the sea or to avoid military service. (Serving as a sailor was a protected occupation in the United States.) For them it was an occupation, not a cause, and they were generally uninterested in fighting. Sailors seeking a fight enlisted.

Unlike the Kriegsmarine *Seemänner*, US Navy personnel aboard cargo ships were almost universally hostilities-only men. The officers came from reserve programs, the enlisted men usually straight out of boot camp or training schools. Oftentimes they were men available when a posting to a ship became open or shifted to the US Navy Armed Guard because they did not fit into the traditional navy.

In the 1940s American men were scrappers. It was part of their tradition growing up. While some were willing tamely to submit when confronted with a superior foe, others were prepared to fight regardless of the odds against them, even when to do so was not part of the job. If they lost the fight, they were content so long as the other guy, even those in an enemy warship, knew he had been in a fight afterward.

THE KRIEGSMARINE RAIDER *SEEMANN*

The Kriegsmarine dated to the creation of the Kaiserliche Marine (Imperial German Navy), formed in 1871. By 1939 the Kaiserliche Marine had changed its name twice: to Reichsmarine in 1919 and Kriegsmarine in 1935. Yet it was the same organization. Most senior Kriegsmarine officers in World War II started their service in the Kaiserliche Marine and were combat veterans of World War I.

The Kriegsmarine was an all-volunteer service before and during World War II. Compared to the Wehrmacht or Luftwaffe, its manpower demands were small. Recruits joined the Kriegsmarine between 17 and 23 years old, but those aged under 21 needed parental permission to do so. Recruits had to be physically fit, in good health (including good teeth), and of at least average intelligence. They also had to demonstrate German nationality, and that they had completed secondary education. A criminal record barred enlistment. Applicants came from all over Germany, inland and coastal regions.

Those who served in the German merchant marine or possessed appropriate technical skills (including completed apprenticeships) in mechanics and electricity were preferred, but the small size of the Kriegsmarine allowed the service to choose with care those who joined. Prewar high unemployment rates in Germany and those preferring naval rather than army service once the war started ensured there was a surplus of applicants.

Recruits joined for at least five years (including a year of training). Kriegsmarine recruits were assigned one of 12 specialties, which ranged from seaman to coastal artillery. Half the recruits became seamen. Others specialized in the skills needed in engine rooms, to man the helm, operate the weapons and communications, or administer paperwork. Some became medical orderlies or musicians.

Kriegsmarine recruits went through the same basic training as Wehrmacht infantry, including wearing Army *Feldgrau* (field gray) uniforms, infantry drill, and weapons training. After completing training they moved on to specialist training schools in Kiel, Mürwick, or Swinemünde, after which they went to service assignments. Trained recruits earned the rank *Matrose* (ordinary seaman). Following a year's service, a

Kriegsmarine officers and sailors inspect the crew and passengers of a ship stopped by a German warship. These confrontations were common in the actions between German surface raiders and Allied merchant ships. (Author's Collection)

A communications *Obergefreiter* (seaman second class) records a radio message broadcast. The enlisted personnel of the Kriegsmarine were volunteers. They were physically fit and generally of above-average intelligence. Those with civilian technical skills were preferred for enlistment. (Author's Collection)

Matrose could expect promotion to *Matrosengefreiter* (able seaman). Long-service men, with at least five years' service as a *Matrosengefreiter*, could receive promotion to *Matrosenhauptgefreiter* (high able seaman). The rank carried no extra pay or responsibility, but conferred extra respect and prestige.

Promotion to *Maat* (petty officer) required an officer's recommendation. Men accepting this promotion lengthened their career obligation to 12 years. During wartime or periods of rapid expansion, promising recruits could be offered an opportunity to become a *Maat* after basic training. Those accepting the promotion after completing basic training went on to their specialist training first. Every *Maat* candidate went to the Marineunteroffizierlehrabteilung (petty-officer school) at either Friedrichsort or (after 1938) Wesermünde in Bremerhaven. They went through the leadership and combat training given army NCOs, again donning *Feldgrau* uniforms, and experienced simulated land combat as part of training.

After three years a *Maat* could receive promotion to *Obermaat*. Senior enlisted personnel could become warrant officers (equivalent to senior petty officers in the US Navy and Royal Navy). There were three career tracks available: one for deck personnel, one for navigation specialists, and one for shore-based personnel. These men were the backbone of a Kriegsmarine ship. The most senior warrant ranks were given to those considered good enough to retain upon completing their 12-year service obligation.

Kaiserliche Marine officers were drawn from Germany's patrician and upper-middle classes. Kaiserliche Marine veterans dominated the upper ranks of the Reichsmarine and Kriegsmarine. Officers who joined the service after 1919 came from more egalitarian backgrounds, passing through a recruitment process similar to those for enlisted personnel. Along with demonstrating a German background, officer candidates also had to provide information on their parents and grandparents.

Officer training was rigorous. Kriegsmarine officers were expected to be competent seamen and navigators as well as leaders. They went through the same basic training as *Matrosen*, followed by four months of practical training, aligned with their career specialty. Officers could be an *Offizier zur See* (line officer), *Ingenieur* (engineering officer), *Waffen-Offizier* (weapons specialist), or a member of the administrative staff. Upon completion of their training, they were promoted to cadet, and served nine months on a training ship. This was followed by 18 months of advanced training for line and engineering candidates (two years for gunnery officers), followed by six months of fleet service. Only then were they promoted to *Leutnant* (lieutenant – equivalent to a US Navy ensign). The subsequent promotion sequence was *Oberleutnant* (lieutenant JG), *Kapitänleutnant* (lieutenant), *Korvettenkapitän* (lieutenant commander), *Fregattenkapitän* (commander), and *Kapitän zur See* (captain). In World War II, Kriegsmarine auxiliary cruisers were commanded by a *Korvettenkapitän*, *Fregattenkapitän*, or *Kapitän zur See*.

The Kriegsmarine was largely apolitical while commanded by Großadmiral Erich Raeder, from its creation in May 1935 until Raeder stepped down in January 1943. During that period Kriegsmarine officers were prohibited from being members of a political party. Officer candidates in the Nazi Party had to resign their membership before accepting a Kriegsmarine commission.

German naval officers and sailors viewed themselves as defenders of the Fatherland, regardless of the party in power. The Kriegsmarine viewed honorable behavior seriously. While determined to defeat the Allied forces, Kriegsmarine personnel maintained great respect for their British and American opponents. They fought hard, but viewed their maritime foes as fellow mariners and adversaries, rather than enemies.

The Kriegsmarine entered World War II with experienced, well-trained crews and a professional, technically competent officer corps. Its members believed they belonged to an elite branch of Germany's armed forces. Rations and living conditions were considered better than in the Wehrmacht, and members generally went into battle having slept in their own bed and eaten a hot meal. Despite Germany's naval buildup between 1935 and 1939, the Kriegsmarine was still relatively small when the war started. It remained relatively small despite the expansion of its U-boat force. U-boats had small crews, and the increase in the number of U-boats was matched by a decrease in the number of large warships with very large crews.

RIGHT
Kriegsmarine officers were drawn from men with leadership ability. They were expected to be competent seamen and navigators as well as leaders, and went through extensive academic and practical training to earn their commissions. (Author's Collection)

FAR RIGHT
Kapitän zur See Horst Gerlach. (NARA)

48

HORST GERLACH

Horst Gerlach, who commanded the German auxiliary cruiser *Stier* during World War II, was born on August 11, 1900, in Erfurt, a town in central Germany. Despite growing up in a landlocked home town, Gerlach wanted a naval career. He joined the Kaiserliche Marine in 1916, initially attending the Marineschule Mürwik (Mürwik Naval Academy) in Flensburg, the training establishment for all Kaiserliche Marine officers. He was posted to the battlecruiser *Seydlitz* in 1917, and promoted to *Leutnant* in 1918.

Gerlach left the Reichsmarine shortly after World War I ended. He rejoined on October 1, 1933, when the establishment of the Kriegsmarine and its subsequent expansion created a need for more officers. Before World War II started he served on the staff at Kriegsmarine headquarters in Berlin as a *Korvettenkapitän*.

After war broke out, in November 1939 Gerlach was promoted to *Fregattenkapitän* and given command of *Uhlenhorst*, a trawler converted to an ASW vessel. In March 1940 he relinquished command of *Uhlenhorst* to take command of *Schiff 23*, formerly the freighter MS *Cairo*, then serving as a Kriegsmarine picket in the Baltic Sea. In April 1941 he took the ship to Schiedam, Netherlands, with orders to supervise its conversion to an auxiliary cruiser. Conversion work was completed on November 11, 1941, and the ship commissioned as a Kriegsmarine warship, with Gerlach commanding. As was Kriegsmarine custom for auxiliary cruisers, the ship was renamed when commissioned as a warship, with its captain selecting the name. Gerlach chose *Stier* ("bull") to honor his wife, Hildegard, whose zodiac sign was Taurus, the bull. By then he was a *Kapitän zur See*, promoted on June 1.

Gerlach proved to be *Stier*'s only captain, commanding the ship on its first cruise, from May through September 27, 1942, when it was scuttled due to damage received from *Stephen Hopkins*. During the cruise Gerlach and *Stier* sank four ships; three freighters, and one tanker.

After the battle with *Stephen Hopkins* Gerlach returned to Nazi-occupied Europe aboard the supply ship *Tannenfels*, along with *Stier*'s surviving crew. He was awarded the German Cross in Gold for the cruise. It was a mark of some disfavor, however, as it was a lower award than the Knight's Cross given to every other Kriegsmarine auxiliary cruiser captain upon completion of a cruise.

Stier was Gerlach's last seagoing command. Thereafter he served in administrative posts. From March 1943 through August 1943, he was the naval district commander Petersburg (the Russian Baltic coast). In September 1943 he transferred to the Mediterranean where he served as naval district commander in the Peloponnesus until September 1944. In November 1944 he was moved to the Netherlands, and became naval district commander, North Holland. He held that position until war's end, in May 1945. All three positions were lateral moves, with no increase in responsibility. Nor did he receive further promotion during the war, a sign of likely disfavor. He survived the war, and was discharged from the Kriegsmarine on March 2, 1946. He died on June 18, 1970, aged 69.

The men and officers who manned the auxiliary cruisers the Kriegsmarine sent out as concealed surface raiders tended to be the best the service had. They were capable of operating independently for long periods of time. Auxiliary cruiser captains were carefully screened, chosen for their competence and independence. Three were captains of sailing training ships prewar; another was a survey ship captain.

In some ways, auxiliary cruisers were manned in a manner similar to 18th- and early 19th-century warships. The captains chose the crews of the ships they commanded. Many took men from ships they had previously commanded. The sailors were volunteers, signing on to the ship for one cruise, rather than simply being assigned to a ship. Most, even for the surface raiders sent out in 1942, were experienced sailors, frequently long-service prewar regulars, rather than wartime recruits. They were generally a cut above the typical Kriegsmarine sailor of 1942, in competence and experience. The Kriegsmarine had to send its best.

THE AMERICAN MERCHANT MARINER

Two groups manned US Merchant Marine ships during World War II: the US Navy Armed Guard manning the guns aboard an armed merchantman, and the crew operating the ship. The Armed Guard were detailed to protect the ship. The crew was made up of civilians who had responsibility of running the ship, although many volunteered to assist the naval guardsmen. The size of both groups varied, depending on the size of the vessel and the number of guns it carried. Typically, an oceangoing merchantman had 38–62 civilian mariners, and 21–40 naval guardsmen. While they shared the same ship and similar skills, they had different backgrounds.

Prewar, the US Navy consisted of highly professional long-service sailors in both enlisted and officer ranks. The Navy – a highly technical service in the mid-20th century – had higher physical and mental standards for enlistment than the US Army because it required capable personnel. The Navy offered better living conditions than the Army, with opportunities to learn skills that would be transferable to peacetime employment.

During the Great Depression, when civilian jobs were scarce, the US Navy was selective of those permitted to enlist; only allowing the best to re-enlist. After World War II began in 1939 the Navy anticipated the entry of the United States into the conflict, and began a massive expansion program which vastly increased numbers of both enlisted and commissioned personnel. Prewar officers and men served as a cadre for the wartime Navy with its reserve officers and wartime enlistees. Enlistment remained voluntary through 1942. US Navy Armed Guard personnel were largely drawn from officers commissioned and men who enlisted during the expansion.

Training began when an individual entered the US Navy and ended when he left. All men who enlisted in the Navy began their careers at Navy Boot Camp, which, during World War II, ran for 4–8 weeks. Recruits were issued uniform and kit (including a copy of *The Bluejackets' Manual*) and learned the fundamentals of being a sailor: basic drill, seamanship, naval customs and courtesy, small-arms training, swimming, and how to live aboard ship.

Upon graduation, new seamen were either assigned directly to ships, where they learned their duties through what was essentially an apprenticeship, or to a school to receive specialty training. There were three categories of schools. Class A schools provided elementary instruction to recruits in technical fields and gave them the groundwork necessary to move into the lowest petty-officer ratings. Class B schools gave enlisted men more advanced instruction in advanced machinery. Class C schools were more advanced still, providing training in subjects not normally a part of shipboard instruction.

Prior to World War II, US Navy officers were largely long-serving, professional men. Officers were expected to be gentlemen as well as mariners. They were expected to have a college education, and serve as leaders. Most were graduates of the United States Naval Academy at Annapolis, Maryland. With the expansion of the fleet, which began in 1935, the Navy realized this corps was too small for intended growth. In response, it initiated a Reserve Officer Training Corps (ROTC) system at US colleges and universities. Upon graduation students received naval training that earned them

a reserve commission with their baccalaureate degrees. This included men attending maritime academies learning to serve as merchant marine officers. During World War II, ROTC training expanded, including the V-7 program in June 1940. V-7 candidates attended college, went through an eight-month United States Naval Reserve Midshipmen's School, and received an ensign's commission upon graduation. V-12 midshipmen attended civilian colleges, supplementing that education with roughly 12 months' training to become a naval officer.

Officers and men assigned to the US Navy Armed Guard were generally drawn from reserve programs. Regular Navy officers and senior petty officers and chiefs were sent to the Navy's growing fleet of regular warships. While less experienced, reserves were professional and highly motivated. Those in the Armed Guard were selected because they were capable of effective action while operating independently.

Merchant mariners came from a different pool than those of the US Navy Armed Guard. They were civilians who signed aboard a ship voluntarily, meaning that in theory they could quit any time or refuse to sign aboard a ship offering a berth. If they did so, however, they lost their draft exemption – and in 1941–42 that meant potential conscription into the US Army.

The mariners in the US Merchant Marine were employed by US-based shipping companies, not the US government. (In some cases, US Merchant Marine ships were owned by US-based companies but sailed under flags of convenience, such as those of Panama and Liberia.) By 1942 pay rates were regulated by the US government to prevent companies from bidding up salaries in search of scarce seamen.

ABOVE LEFT

Merchant mariners were all civilian and volunteers. The vast increase in the size of the US Merchant Marine fleet led to shortages of trained seamen. This poster was intended to encourage recruiting. (Library of Congress)

ABOVE RIGHT

The US Merchant Marine mariner was a civilian. He took to the sea as a job. He did not wear a uniform and was not viewed as a combatant, although he ran the same risks as men in the US Army and US Navy. (Library of Congress)

Two classes of mariners served aboard US-owned or US-flagged merchant vessels: licensed and unlicensed. Licensed mariners had licenses issued or recognized by the US government. They represented a ship's officer and leadership cadre. Unlicensed mariners made up the rest of the crew. They varied in skill from highly experienced and skilled individuals to entry-level sailors, undertaking their first voyage. Positions above entry level required certifications qualifying the individual for their role.

In 1942 there were three tracks for unlicensed mariners: deck, engine, or steward. The deck crew dealt with loading and unloading cargo, serving deck watch, and steering the ship. The engine-room crew operated the ship's engines. The steward's division undertook housekeeping duties, including meal preparation. Most training for these positions occurred on the job.

Ship's officers were all licensed. By 1940 all but the oldest had attended a state maritime academy or the US Maritime Academy. These academies trained merchant officers and provided a baccalaureate-degree upon graduation. Schooling included tours aboard merchant vessels as cadets before graduation for practical experience. Officers specialized in deck or engineering tracks. Promotion followed a path similar to that of naval officers. Experience gained promotion to positions of greater responsibility, culminating as chief engineer for the engineering track or as a ship's master, holding a master mariner's license.

Even before World War II began, the US Merchant Marine experienced significant growth. After the war began, US shipyards began mass-producing merchant vessels,

EDWIN JOSEPH O'HARA

Edwin Joseph O'Hara was born on November 27, 1923, in Lindsay, California, the youngest son of Joseph C. and Elma F. O'Hara. Edwin's father grew oranges in a grove in California's Central Valley where his son grew up.

In late 1941 Edwin was accepted into the cadet program at the US Merchant Marine Academy. Ten days after his 18th birthday Japan bombed Pearl Harbor; he was determined to serve, preferably in the US Navy as a submariner. Because of his age and lack of college education, he realized the fastest way to get into a commissioned position was to become a US Merchant Marine officer, continuing with the US Merchant Marine Academy.

Due to the war, the US Maritime Commission opened a cadet training school on Treasure Island in San Francisco Bay, which commissioned US Merchant Marine officers in an accelerated program. It had an eight-week basic course, followed by nine months at sea as a cadet, after which the cadets completed nine months of classwork to become licensed officers. O'Hara opted for this, entering the school in January 1942 and completing his basic training in March.

O'Hara was assigned sea duty aboard the troopship SS *Mariposa* on March 14, 1942. A knee injury, infected while he was aboard, forced him to leave *Mariposa* on May 3 when it returned to San Francisco. He switched from deck officer specialization to engine officer specialization, and spent the next two weeks recovering from the infection.

On May 16 O'Hara signed on to a just-launched Liberty ship, SS *Stephen Hopkins*, which was beginning its maiden voyage. He served in the engine room as an officer cadet. He was fascinated by guns, and was one of the civilian crew aboard *Stephen Hopkins* who volunteered to serve the ship's guns. He spent his free time on the voyage across the Pacific to Bora Bora and New Zealand and then across the Indian Ocean to Cape Town drilling with the crew of the aft 4in gun.

When the Kriegsmarine auxiliary cruiser *Stier* attacked *Stephen Hopkins* early in the morning of September 27, O'Hara was in the engine room. After the engine room was hit and its crew forced to clear it, he went up to the deck. He saw a 15cm shell strike near the 4in/50 gun, killing its crew. When a second large-caliber shell hit a lifeboat being lowered from *Stephen Hopkins*, he ran to the gun to resume firing it. He did this to draw German fire away from the lifeboats.

Reaching the gun, O'Hara cleared the dead bodies away from it. Five shells remained in the ready locker. He single-handedly loaded the five 64lb rounds into the gun, and fired it at the ship at which it was most closely aimed, the supply ship *Tannenfels*. He fired all five rounds before being killed by a burst of automatic fire from one of *Stier*'s light guns.

Engine Cadet O'Hara was posthumously awarded the Merchant Marine Distinguished Service Medal for his conduct. A Liberty ship named for him, SS *Edwin Joseph O'Hara*, was launched on July 29, 1943. The US Merchant Marine Academy at Kings Point, NY, later named an athletics hall after him.

resulting in an unprecedented increase in demand for merchant mariners. The state maritime academies expanded their programs to increase the number of officers and licensed mariners found themselves holding positions requiring far greater seniority to fill than during the 1920s and early 1930s. Ships filled crews with anyone remotely qualified, including foreign sailors. The Luckenbach Steamship Company signed several Greek sailors for service on *Stephen Hopkins*, only one of whom spoke English. He had to translate orders to the others. This was not unusual.

Merchant mariners were technically noncombatants. They were civilians, with the guns aboard the ships manned by naval personnel due to international law and custom. In practice, the merchant crew aboard served the guns during combat on a voluntary basis. In combat, they suffered the same fate as the US Navy Armed Guard personnel aboard – motivation enough for merchant mariners to participate in hope of preserving their ship.

COMBAT

Germany's first wave of surface raiders ended operations in November 1941, a few weeks before the United States entered World War II. It had been a successful campaign, with 99 Allied vessels captured or sunk. Even as that wave was cresting, however, the Kriegsmarine was preparing to send out a second wave of auxiliary cruisers.

Only two of the first wave's seven surface raiders (*Thor* and *Komet*) were available for another raider cruise by December 1941. Three (*Atlantis*, *Pinguin*, and *Kormoran*) had been sunk after battle with Royal Navy cruisers. The two oldest merchantmen converted to auxiliary cruisers (*Orion* and *Widder*, both launched in 1930) were worn out and incapable of another cruise. Additionally, *Widder*'s engines were unreliable. It needed to stay close to home.

The Kriegsmarine was converting two more merchantmen into auxiliary cruisers during 1941 as replacements: *Cairo*, formerly a civilian freighter before being requisitioned by the Kriegsmarine on November 9, 1941, and converted to a minelayer, for which role it was not used, then modified as an auxiliary cruiser in April 1941, would become *Stier*; and *Bonn*, which started life as the freighter *Bielsko* before it was requisitioned by the Kriegsmarine for use as a hospital ship and then commissioned as an auxiliary cruiser on September 7, 1941, would become *Michel*. Along with *Thor* and *Komet*, they took to sea in 1942.

Thor, originally the cargo ship *Santa Cruz* before being requisitioned by the Kriegsmarine in late 1939 and converted as an auxiliary cruiser, in which role it was commissioned on March 15, 1940, was first to depart. On November 20, however, soon after setting out from Kiel at the start of its second cruise, it collided with and sank the Swedish freighter SS *Bothnia* anchored off Brunsbüttel because of dense fog. After repairs at Kiel, it was able to reach the Gironde on December 17, but bad weather kept it in France for a month. *Thor* finally left Gironde on January 14, 1942,

on what was to be a successful nine-month second cruise during which it sank seven ships and took three more as prizes. All the encounters occurred in the South Atlantic, around the Cape of Good Hope and Indian Ocean.

Thor and its three prizes (the Australian liner *Nankin* and the Norwegian tankers *Herborg* and *Madrono*) successfully reached Yokohama, Japan, on October 9, 1942. On November 30, while outfitting in preparation for a third cruise, captured ammunition aboard the German supply ship *Uckermark* exploded. *Thor*, docked next to *Uckermark* in Yokohama Harbor, was showered with flaming debris and caught fire, leaving the auxiliary cruiser unrepairable. *Thor* took no US ships on its second voyage, and exits this study.

Michel took to the sea next, leaving Kiel on March 6, 1942, commanded by Fregattenkapitän Helmuth von Ruckteschell who was on his second raiding voyage. Ruckteschell oversaw *Michel*'s conversion to an auxiliary cruiser, naming it for Archangel Michael. (The antichristian Nazi regime insisted it was named for Deutscher Michel, who personified Germany, like Britain's John Bull.) Ruckteschell, *Widder*'s former commander, had *Widder*'s guns installed on *Michel*, and brought *Widder*'s officers and some of its crew with him. To reach the Atlantic, *Michel* had to transit the Channel. It reached the French port of Saint-Malo after fighting its way through the Channel, narrowly avoiding being torpedoed by Royal Navy motor-torpedo boats. At Saint-Malo it replenished its ammunition, refueled, and departed into the Atlantic on March 20.

Over the next year *Michel* ran wild, sinking 15 ships in 12 months before safely reaching Kobe, Japan, on March 1, 1943. Five of its 15 "kills" (the tankers SS *Connecticut* and SS *William F. Humphrey*, the Liberty ship SS *George Clymer*, the brand-new diesel-engine cargo ship MS *American Leader*, and the 1920s-era MS *Sawokla*) flew the US flag. *Michel* used shellfire to sink *William F. Humphrey* and *American Leader*, and a combination of shellfire and its own torpedoes on *Sawokla*. *Connecticut* and *George Clymer* were sunk by *Esau*, a motor-torpedo boat carried by *Michel*.

Michel undertook a second cruise during May 21–October 17, 1943, sailing from Yokohama under the command of Kapitän zur See Günther Gumprich. *Michel* sank only three ships (the freighter *Høegh Silverdawn* and the tankers *Ferncastle* and *India*; all Norwegian) during the five-month cruise. As *Michel* made its way back to

55

MS *Sawokla* was the last American merchant vessel to be sunk or taken by a German surface raider. It was *Michel*'s thirteenth victim. This photograph was taken shortly after *Sawokla* was converted to diesel propulsion, making it one of the relatively few America motorships. (Author's Collection)

Yokohama on October 17 it was torpedoed and sunk by a US Navy submarine, USS *Tarpon*. A total of 290 crew perished and 116 survived the sinking.

Stier departed Rotterdam on May 9, 1942, as part of a Channel convoy. The convoy fought the length of the Channel, facing shore batteries at Dover and nighttime attacks by Royal Navy motor-torpedo boats. Although *Stier* was undamaged, two escorting E-boats and one Royal Navy motor-torpedo boat were sunk during the running battle. *Stier* broke out into the Atlantic on May 19, shortly after arriving at the French port of Royan on the Channel coast.

Hansa was the last auxiliary cruiser the Kriegsmarine attempted to send to sea. Unable to break into the Atlantic, it spent the rest of the war as a target for training U-boats. Postwar it returned to the Glen Line, its original owners, and resumed service as SS *Glengarry*. (Author's Collection)

BLOCKADE RUNNERS AND SUPPLY SHIPS

Kriegsmarine warships depended on an assortment of Kriegsmarine tankers and supply ships for support when conducting cruises on the open ocean. They were drawn from Germany's merchant marine and requisitioned into the Kriegsmarine either immediately before or during World War II. The Kriegsmarine also used these ships as blockade runners to take critical cargos to and from Nazi-occupied Europe and Japanese territories.

Sometimes these ships switched roles. *Altmark*, the best known of these Kriegsmarine auxiliaries, served as *Admiral Graf Spee*'s supply ship during its 1939 cruise. In 1942 *Altmark* ran a cargo of vegetable oil and fuel to Japan, replenishing the auxiliary cruiser *Michel* during its trip.

Similarly, *Tannenfels*, running a cargo of critical metals from Japan to France, rendezvoused in the South Atlantic to refuel *Stier*.

There were never many of these supply ships, certainly fewer than two dozen. Only a dozen were in commission and rarely more than six actually at sea at one time. They were critical to auxiliary cruiser success, however, because they extended the range and duration of a cruise, simultaneously providing a friendly contact for the crews on isolated duty. While they ran the same risks and faced the same dangers as auxiliary cruisers, they rarely received recognition for the risks they ran supporting them.

Stier had a short but spectacular career. It sank only four ships, including two American vessels, the Panamanian-flagged tanker *Stanvac Calcutta* and the Liberty ship *Stephen Hopkins*. Both resisted fiercely, although *Stanvac Calcutta*'s gunnery proved ineffective. *Stephen Hopkins* achieved much better results, damaging *Stier* badly enough that it was scuttled by its crew after *Stephen Hopkins* sank.

Komet's turn came on October 7, 1942, when it departed Vlissingen disguised as a minesweeper. As with *Michel* and *Stier*, it had to fight its way down the Channel. It reached Dunkirk safely, but British intelligence identified it as a surface raider. When it departed Dunkirk on October 12, it sailed into a trap set by the Royal Navy in which four groups of warships covered the routes to Le Havre. *Komet* ran into one group, and was torpedoed and sunk by a motor-torpedo boat.

Two other naval auxiliaries were converted into auxiliary cruisers during 1942 and 1943. *Togo*, launched in 1938, was serving as a fighter-direction ship after being requisitioned by the Kriegsmarine until chosen for conversion. *Hansa*, a war prize

Blockade runner *Odenwald* was seized by the US Navy in the South Atlantic on November 6, 1941. (US Naval History and Heritage Command)

seized in Copenhagen when Germany occupied Denmark, was originally under construction for a British shipping line. Launched in 1939, it was serving as a target ship for U-boat training. Neither vessel was able to break through the Channel and both were assigned other duties for the war's duration.

STANVAC CALCUTTA VS STIER, JUNE 6, 1942

On the morning of June 6, 1942, T2 tanker *Stanvac Calcutta* was 500NM off Recife, Brazil, steaming north to Caripito, Venezuela, to load petroleum. It was a new ship, built the previous year to service Stanvac's Far East oil trade. Stanvac, a joint venture between Socony-Vacuum Oil Company and Standard Oil of New Jersey (today both are part of Exxon-Mobile), had been expanding its business there prior to the Japanese attack on Pearl Harbor, after which the war prevented *Stanvac Calcutta* from being used as intended. Instead, the WSA requisitioned it in April 1941 and assigned it to carry product in the South Atlantic.

While under WSA charter, *Stanvac Calcutta* was still owned and operated by Stanvac, maintaining a Stanvac crew and its master, Captain Gustaf Karlsson. The tanker had a nine-man naval guard aboard and was hastily armed with what could be scrounged when requisitioned. In this case it was a 4in/50 gun aft, a 3in/23 gun forward, and four .50 machine guns. The 3in/23 was a World War I-era antiaircraft version of the 3in gun, abandoned by the US Navy and available as surplus.

Stanvac Calcutta was returning from Montevideo, Uruguay, in ballast. The seas were rough, filled with rainstorms and overcast skies. At 1012hrs, a ship appeared out of a rain squall, 4NM to port. It was the auxiliary cruiser *Stier*. Its lookouts spotted a tanker, a big one, before *Stier* was seen by the tanker. It was potentially *Stier*'s second victim. Two days earlier, *Stier* had found and sunk the British freighter SS *Gemstone*, headed to Baltimore from South Africa with a load of iron ore. *Gemstone* surrendered after a brief attempt at flight. *Stier*'s commander, Kapitän zur See Horst Gerlach, expected the same to happen this time. The unidentified tanker was still in its peacetime livery and he believed it to be an unarmed merchantman.

The unidentified tanker would be a valuable prize, especially if it carried diesel. Because tankers carried volatile cargos, they were vulnerable to gunfire and frequently surrendered when approached. It was worth attempting to capture this tanker rather than sink it. Gerlach unmasked his guns and fired a warning shot. *Stier* signaled, using International Code, "Stop Your Engines." Then *Stier* commenced radio jamming to prevent the tanker transmitting a warning.

At first, Karlsson and First Mate Aage Knudsen believed the ship that had emerged from the rain squall was British, and they ordered the Panamanian flag hoisted as a response. Then both men took a closer look, using binoculars, and realized the other ship was flying a German naval ensign: it was a German surface raider.

The armament *Stanvac Calcutta* carried was adequate to chase off a U-boat, but not an auxiliary cruiser. *Stier* had a broadside of four 15cm SK L/45 guns and one 53.3cm underwater torpedo tube. Regardless, Karlsson refused meekly to surrender and took his ship into action.

Perhaps Karlsson might have yielded if *Stanvac Calcutta* had been loaded, especially had it been carrying volatile gasoline. One or two hits would have set the tanker ablaze. Crude oil or bunker fuel used by steamships was less explosive, but it would still burn. The tanker was in ballast, however. Its tanks were empty, purged of volatile gases after unloading its cargo in Montevideo. It had plenty of reserve buoyancy. Unless hit in its engine spaces, steering gear, or bridge decks, shellfire would do relatively little damage. Under those circumstances the fight was far more even. Karlsson probably felt he had a reasonable chance of driving off the surface raider or perhaps landing a lucky hit that might cripple it. *Stanvac Calcutta* could take more damage than a surface raider.

Karlsson ordered *Stanvac Calcutta* ahead full, and turned to starboard, to allow both guns to bear on the raider. He sent the crew to battle stations. The US Navy Armed Guard, nine men under the command of Ensign Edward L. Anderson, manned the stern 4in/50 gun. Volunteers from the crew took the bow 3in/23 gun. They had been drilling for two months.

Guns aboard American merchantmen were manned by units from the US Navy Armed Guard. These men were assisted on a volunteer basis by members of the civilian crew. The men shown here manned the guns of the Liberty ship SS *John Mason*. (US Naval History and Heritage Command)

A furious 15-minute exchange of gunfire occurred. Once he realized his chance to capture the tanker was gone, Gerlach opened fire with every gun *Stier* had: four 15cm SK L/45 guns firing 100lb rounds with each salvo, augmented by the 3.7cm and two 2cm autocannons that could be brought to bear. The big guns concentrated on *Stanvac Calcutta*'s engine spaces and 4in/50 gun aft and the bridge amidships. The lighter guns attempted to suppress the crews manning the guns. The tanker responded in kind, with both bow and stern guns.

Stier landed multiple hits on *Stanvac Calcutta* that destroyed the bridge and radio room, killing Karlsson, the helmsman, and the radio operator. Another hit destroyed the sights on the stern gun. In all, *Stier* fired 148 15cm rounds, 3rd/min from each gun. Yet the tanker's gun crews stuck to their task. They got off 20–30 shots, the stern gun continuing to fire even after the sights were blown off. The 4in/50 gun ran out of ready ammunition; Anderson sent a party below to get more. The 3in/23 bow gun fired fewer rounds because some of the elderly rounds misfired. The bad rounds had to be cleared before firing could resume.

Stanvac Calcutta landed only two hits on *Stier*, both most likely fired by the stern gun. One hit the foremast; the second exploded in the crew quarters aft of the No. 5 hatch, injuring two of *Stier*'s crew. *Stier*'s gunfire failed to stop the tanker, however. Wishing to bring the battle to an end, Gerlach fired a torpedo at the tanker. It hit, causing flooding and killing several other members of the crew. The tanker began listing. Knudsen, overseeing damage control, attempted to shift ballast to correct the list. Unsuccessful, he returned to the bridge for orders, only to find Karlsson dead. With the tanker sinking, the surviving crew abandoned ship.

Stier picked up survivors. Of the 51 crew and naval guard aboard *Stanvac Calcutta*, 13 were killed during the battle; a fourteenth man died of wounds, the next day, while aboard *Stier*. Several more men were wounded. One seaman, Saedie B. Hassan, was so badly wounded he remained hospitalized on *Stier*. *Stanvac Calcutta's* survivors along with the crew of *Gemstone* were transferred to the Kriegsmarine supply ship *Charlotte Schliemann* two days later on June 10. Some were later transferred to *Doggerbank*, another supply ship. Both sets of prisoners were eventually landed in Japan, spending the rest of the war in Japanese POW camps. One died in captivity.

Hassan was luckier. Transferred to *Tannenfels*, he ended up in France, and recovered in a French hospital. Later he was sent to Milag Nord POW camp in Germany, from where he was released in April 1945. Unlike the prisoners in Japan, held incommunicado, the Germans allowed Hassan to write. Having no relatives he sent his letter to Stanvac headquarters. He notified them of *Stanvac Calcutta's* loss and asked for size 6½ shoes and cigarettes. His letter arrived on March 13, 1943. By then *Stanvac Calcutta* had been overdue, presumed lost with all hands, for nine months. Death indemnities had been paid to families and had to be recovered.

Michel made most of its attacks at night, like the one shown here. This attack was photographed from the decks of one of the auxiliary cruisers sent out in 1940. (Author's Collection)

GEORGE CLYMER VS MICHEL AND ESAU, JUNE 6, 1942

The same day *Stier* sank *Stanvac Calcutta*, Fregattenkapitän Helmuth von Ruckteschell's *Michel* attacked the Liberty ship SS *George Clymer*, leading to its sinking. *Michel* did not directly attack *George Clymer*, however. Rather it was torpedoed by *LS-4*, *Michel's* torpedo boat.

Ruckteschell was Germany's most experienced auxiliary cruiser commander by 1942. He used every opportunity to minimize risk when seeking Allied merchant shipping. Frequently, before attacking with *Michel*, he sent one of its Ar 196 floatplanes to attack first, removing a victim's radio aerials by trailing a grapple behind the aircraft. This prevented a warning message being radioed out.

Ruckteschell also made extensive use of *Michel's* torpedo boat. Dubbed *Esau* by

Michel's crew, it was armed with two 45cm torpedo tubes and a 2cm autocannon in a power turret. It carried F5b torpedoes, normally used by aircraft. Sea conditions permitting, if Ruckteschell learned of a potential target he used *Esau* to attack it first.

Rather than the dramatic high-speed torpedo run beloved by Hollywood, *Esau* typically attacked at a crawl. *Michel* trailed its prey, unseen, until darkness fell. *Esau* was then lowered into the water. It approached its prey slowly, leaving no wake. A small visual target when approaching head-on and low in the water, the torpedo boat was almost impossible for a lookout to spot at night. Unseen, once close enough, it fired its torpedoes into an unsuspecting ship, usually to spectacular result.

The first victim to fall prey to these tactics was the US-flagged T2 tanker *Connecticut*. Launched in 1938 it was owned by Texaco and under WSA charter. It was carrying a mixed load of gasoline and fuel oil from Port Arthur, Texas, to Cape Town, South Africa, when spotted by *Michel* in the South Atlantic. As night fell, Ruckteschell ordered *Esau* lowered into the water. It gained a firing position, launching two torpedoes at the tanker in the early hours of April 22, 1942.

The first torpedo struck *Connecticut* at 0210hrs. The tanker's crew promptly abandoned ship. They had just gotten their lifeboats in the water when the second torpedo launched by *Esau* struck. *Connecticut's* cargo exploded. Two of the three lifeboats were caught in the fireball. *Michel* recovered 19 survivors from the third lifeboat, one of whom died later. It was *Michel's* second kill. Three days earlier it had used gunfire to sink the British-flagged Shell tanker SS *Patella*.

Six weeks later, with the Norwegian freighter MV *Kattegat* having been sunk on May 20, it was the freighter *George Clymer's* turn. *Michel* did not have to find *George Clymer*. The Liberty ship advertised its position.

Crews of Kriegsmarine warships worked together as a team. Those sent out on auxiliary cruisers were men capable of acting autonomously and able to deal with the isolation the detached service aboard a surface raider required.

(Author's Collection)

Built by the Oregon Shipbuilding Company and launched on February 19, 1942, *George Clymer* was carrying a load of timber and aircraft from Portland, Oregon, to Cape Town, South Africa, for the American Mail Line. Its voyage had been unremarkable until it entered the South Atlantic. On May 31 its propeller shaft thrust bearing split 600NM southwest of Ascension Island, rendering it immobile. The necessary repairs were beyond the capabilities of the crew.

George Clymer, having drifted for two days, finally sent out a distress message on June 2. The message included its position and requested air cover. (It was out of range of Ascension Island, the nearest Allied airfield.) *Michel*, 900NM away, picked up the message. The freighter was a long way off, but Ruckteschell decided to try to find it.

It took *Michel* four days to close range on *George Clymer* and then to find it. The freighter had drifted 200NM since *Michel* intercepted its June 2 radio plea. Ruckteschell conducted a search to find it. He was half-convinced the derelict was a trap – it seemed too convenient – so he proceeded cautiously when approaching his quarry. He decided to have *Esau* scout out the situation before bringing *Michel* within sight of the ship he was hunting. As evening fell on June 6, he lowered *Esau* into the water.

As with the attack on *Connecticut*, *Esau* waited for full dark, and approached *George Clymer* slowly to prevent kicking up a wake. Since the target was motionless, it was easily stalked. Its high profile was easily visible against the nighttime sky. June is winter in the Southern Hemisphere, so by 2100hrs it was dark enough for *Esau* to move in. Finally it was in a firing position and launched both of its torpedoes.

George Clymer's crew had been experiencing a boring, but comfortable existence aboard the stationary Liberty ship. They had power, electricity, and adequate water and stores. The engine ran. The freighter just could not move anywhere except as ocean currents took it. After five days at the whim of winds, the crew had become complacent. The lookouts were not as alert as they should have been.

At 2200hrs a torpedo slammed into *George Clymer*'s port hull amidships, flooding the boiler room and engine room. A few seconds later the second torpedo hit the hull at the aft end of Hold 1. The crew did not spot *Esau*, which withdrew as unobtrusively as it had approached. They assumed a U-boat had torpedoed them. With the freighter listing ominously to port and perhaps fearing a third torpedo hit from the nonexistent U-boat, the crew panicked. They took to the lifeboats in such haste, the naval guard and two members of the engine gang were stranded aboard.

As dawn broke the next morning, *George Clymer* was still afloat. At 0800hrs the crew reboarded the ship. Their reunion with those left stranded must have been interesting. Later that morning a patrolling Allied aircraft overflew the freighter, signaling help was on the way. A Royal Navy armed merchant cruiser, HMS *Alcantara*, had been previously dispatched to salvage the freighter. It arrived at 1600hrs on June 7.

The original plan was to tow *George Clymer* to safety, but the report it had been torpedoed by a U-boat altered arrangements. The risk to *Alcantara* by towing a freighter which had a mechanical failure across an empty South Atlantic was low, but towing would make the British merchant cruiser highly vulnerable to U-boat attack. *Alcantara* was ordered to sink the derelict.

OVERLEAF

George Clymer, a Liberty ship laden with timber and aircraft from the American northwest, broke down in the South Atlantic on May 30, 1942. Two days later it sent out an SOS picked up by the surface raider *Michel*. Despite suspecting a trap, Fregattenkapitän Helmuth von Ruckteschell, *Michel*'s captain, decided to respond to the call. He crossed the South Atlantic to intercept *George Clymer*. Because Ruckteschell thought it might be a trap, *Michel* did not attack *George Clymer* directly. It did not even come within sight of the freighter. Instead, Ruckteschell unloaded *Esau*, a torpedo boat *Michel* carried, at dusk to seek out and attack *George Clymer* that night. Traveling too slowly to leave a noticeable wake, *Esau* found the Liberty ship at the advertised position. *George Clymer*'s lookouts failed to spot *Esau*. The torpedo boat crept up to *George Clymer* under cover of darkness, launching two torpedoes when close enough not to miss. One hit flooded the engine room. The second struck the after end of Hold 1 a few seconds later. *Esau* withdrew, again unnoticed by *George Clymer*'s lookouts. They believed they had been attacked by a U-boat. This plate shows the scene as the second torpedo strikes home. *Esau* rests in the water unobserved, as it assesses the damage it has inflicted. In the distance flames silhouette *George Clymer*, as its panicked crew hastily lowers the lifeboat lest a freighter filled with timber and deck cargo aircraft explodes and sinks before they get off.

Alcantara took the survivors aboard and began shelling *George Clymer*, which stubbornly refused to sink. *Alcantara* launched its floatplane which dropped depth charges next to *George Clymer*, but still it refused to sink. *Alcantara* remained in the area five days, repeatedly shelling the wreck, but it refused to sink. Finally, on June 12, *Alcantara* abandoned the effort. By then the stricken freighter had capsized. While the derelict remained a hazard to navigation, there were greater hazards in 1942 and *Alcantara* had business elsewhere.

As for *Michel*, the cautious Ruckteschell had hauled off after recovering *Esau*. He planned to return the next day to check the status of his victim. As he returned to the scene, *Michel*'s lookouts spotted a pair of tall masts on the horizon. The unidentified ship was moving swiftly, but its speed and mast tops indicated it was another warship, likely a cruiser hunting German raiders. *Michel*'s radio room intercepted a broadcast from a nearby British ship. It reported *George Clymer* had been torpedoed by a U-boat. Ruckteschell, not seeking an engagement with another warship, broke away, moving in the opposite direction. It proved the wisest course of action. *Michel* would sink 11 more merchantmen (including two more US ships) during a successful cruise that ended with its safe arrival in Japan in March 1943.

STEPHEN HOPKINS VS STIER, SEPTEMBER 27, 1942

Stephen Hopkins was another new cargo ship in 1942. It was launched on April 14 of that year, and started its maiden voyage two months later. On September 27, it was in the South Atlantic, midway between South America and Africa, almost due east of Rio de Janeiro, Brazil, heading homeward from a near circumnavigation of the globe. Starting in California, it had crossed the Pacific and Indian oceans making stops along the way. It had lately left Cape Town in ballast, and was steaming independently for Bahia, Brazil. There it would join a convoy to Paramaribo, Dutch Guiana, where it would load bauxite for its leg back to the United States.

The weather was marginal. Visibility was 1NM at dawn, but by 0800hrs it had improved to 2NM. Then, at 0852hrs two ships loomed out of the rain. Both were large ships with the appearance of merchant vessels. The nearer of the two, the smaller ship, appeared to be heavily armed. It sent a signal using flags: "Stop at Once."

The ships were *Stier*, accompanied by the slightly larger blockade runner *Tannenfels*. They had been in a mid-ocean rendezvous for the previous two days. On its way home after a voyage to Japan *Tannenfels* had resupplied and refueled *Stier*. Members of *Stier*'s crew spent the time repairing a malfunctioning cylinder in its diesel engine, and cleaning and repainting the ship's sides. Men in floats alongside worked until 0800hrs, when they were ordered back aboard due to worsening weather. *Stier* was still stationary when a lookout spotted an approaching ship.

The chance encounter was *Stier*'s good fortune and *Stephen Hopkins*'s bad luck. Had the Liberty ship's course taken it another mile or two distant from *Stier*, it would have passed unnoticed by the Germans and likely made port safely. As it was, Kapitän zur See Horst Gerlach saw an opportunity dropped in his lap, and grabbed it. Since sinking *Stanvac Calcutta* on June 6 *Stier* had found and sunk only one other ship, the British freighter SS *Dalhousie*. That was over a month earlier, on August 9. Gerlach ordered his crew to quarters, unmasked his guns, and signaled the other ship to stop.

Instead of stopping, Captain Paul Buck aboard *Stephen Hopkins* ordered the US colors raised, and commanded the helmsman to turn the ship hard to port. He wanted the stern facing toward the enemy, both to present the smallest possible target and to give his only effective gun, the 4in/50 stern gun, the best field of fire available. He had all the guns manned. Seeing the ship refusing to stop, Gerlach had *Stier* turn to starboard, to expose his full battery. At 0856hrs, both sides opened fire; *Stier* with its 2cm and 3.7cm autocannons, *Stephen Hopkins* with its bow-mounted twin 37mm cannons. One minute later, *Stier*'s four 15cm SK L/45 guns opened up.

Both sides scored hits. The first salvo from *Stier*'s 15cm guns landed a hit amidships, killing two members of *Stephen Hopkins*'s engine-room crew. Two other 15cm shells followed. The freighter scored its first hit at 0900hrs, when shots fired from its 37mm cannons struck *Stier*. Meanwhile *Stier*'s light guns were raking the pilothouse and bridge. Chief Mate Richard Moczkowski was felled by this fire.

Tannenfels, which broke away when *Stephen Hopkins* was sighted, now joined the fight. Seeing *Stier* being fired upon, it asked for permission to fire its guns. Gerlach granted it, and *Tannenfels* began firing at *Stephen Hopkins*. Its fire was inaccurate, however, and missed the freighter.

At 0901hrs *Stephen Hopkins*'s radio officer, Hudson A. Hewey, began broadcasting a "Q" message, repeated Morse "Qs," indicating it was under attack by a disguised warship. *Stier*'s radio jammed the transmission, but the message got through, giving *Stephen Hopkins*'s position. Hewey repeated the alert two more times before being killed by *Stier*'s flak guns.

Stier's main battery was landing hits throughout the first ten minutes of the battle. One of the early shots burst *Stephen Hopkins*'s starboard boiler. The boiler exploded, killing five more members of the engine-room crew. The loss of steam slowed the freighter's speed to 1kt.

At 0905hrs *Stephen Hopkins*'s 4in/50 stern gun opened fire. The gun crew was led by Ensign Kenneth M. Willet, who had drilled the members of the US Navy Armed Guard, and volunteers from the ship's civilian crew, extensively over the previous five months. Among the volunteers was Engine Cadet Edwin J. O'Hara, an 18-year-old from the Merchant Marine Training Academy on Treasure Island, California. Fascinated by the guns, he spent much of his spare time practicing with them.

Willet's Armed Guard crew was superbly trained, and their accuracy was phenomenal. Over a ten-minute period Willet's team fired 35 4in rounds, with 15 of the rounds hitting *Stier*. They knocked out *Stier*'s steering engine, crippling the raider's maneuverability; started fires in several places aboard; and ruptured several oil tanks, the leaking oil feeding the fires. One hit rendered the fire pumps inoperable, leaving the fire hoses without pressure and preventing *Stier*'s damage-control teams from fighting the fires effectively.

At 0910hrs *Stier* ceased firing, to let Gerlach assess the damage his guns had done to *Stephen Hopkins*. It was severe. Nine of the 15-man US Navy Armed Guard crew were dead. The ship had been hit numerous times, and there were a dozen fires burning. The engine room had been evacuated. *Stephen Hopkins* was settling in the water, sinking.

Yet Willet, wounded, continued firing the 4in/50 stern gun. At 0913hrs, Gerlach resumed firing. At 0918hrs one 15cm round landed in *Stephen Hopkins*'s 4in magazine. The magazine exploded, opening up the stern. At 0920hrs, Buck ordered *Stephen Hopkins* abandoned. One man, Edwin O'Hara, stayed aboard. O'Hara, who had been

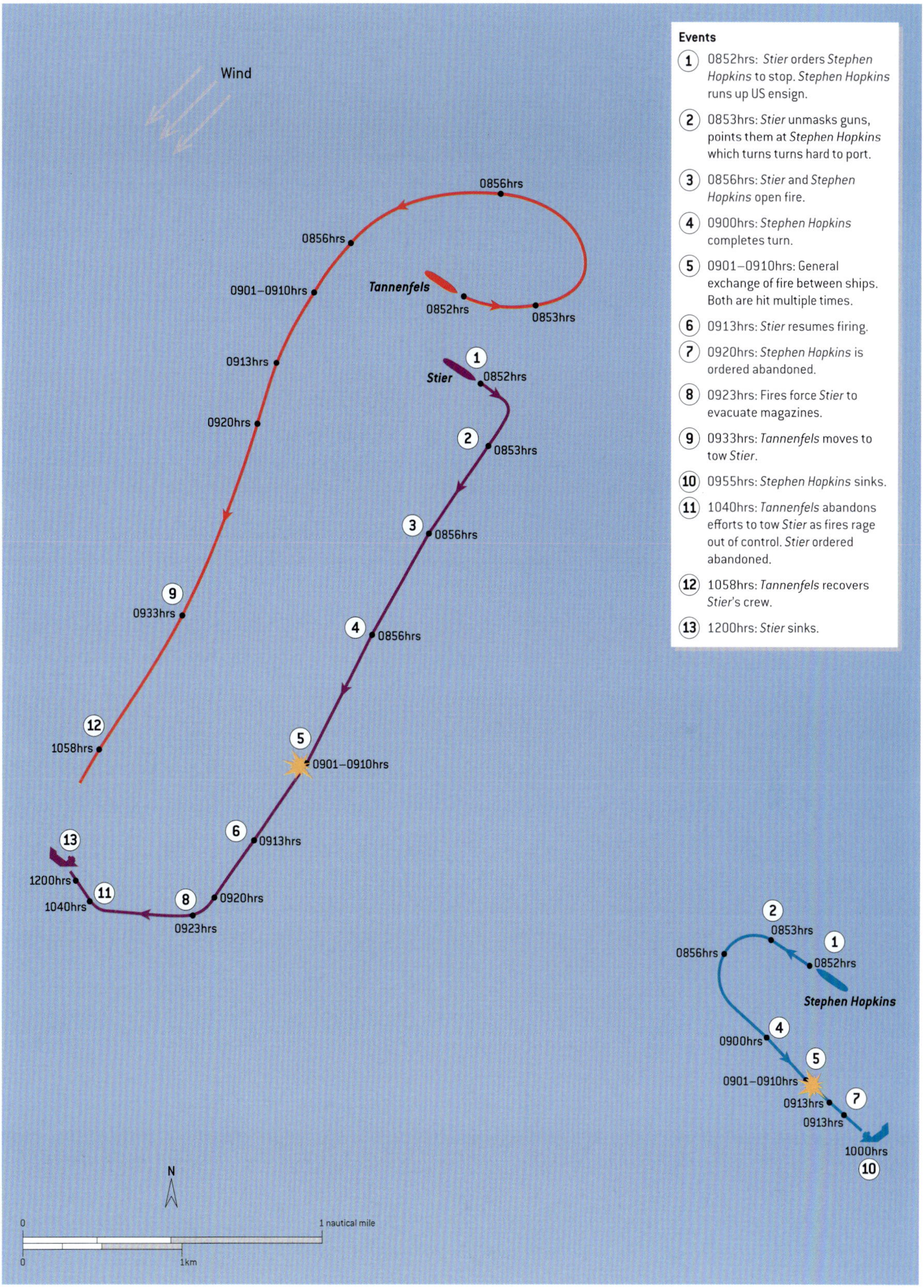

Wind

0856hrs

0856hrs

0901–0910hrs

Tannenfels

0852hrs   0853hrs

0913hrs

0920hrs

1 0852hrs

Stier

2 0853hrs

3 0856hrs

4 0856hrs

9
0933hrs

5 0901–0910hrs

12
1058hrs

6 0913hrs

13
1200hrs
11
1040hrs   **8** 0920hrs
0923hrs

Events

1 0852hrs: *Stier* orders *Stephen Hopkins* to stop. *Stephen Hopkins* runs up US ensign.

2 0853hrs: *Stier* unmasks guns, points them at *Stephen Hopkins* which turns turns hard to port.

3 0856hrs: *Stier* and *Stephen Hopkins* open fire.

4 0900hrs: *Stephen Hopkins* completes turn.

5 0901–0910hrs: General exchange of fire between ships. Both are hit multiple times.

6 0913hrs: *Stier* resumes firing.

7 0920hrs: *Stephen Hopkins* is ordered abandoned.

8 0923hrs: Fires force *Stier* to evacuate magazines.

9 0933hrs: *Tannenfels* moves to tow *Stier*.

10 0955hrs: *Stephen Hopkins* sinks.

11 1040hrs: *Tannenfels* abandons efforts to tow *Stier* as fires rage out of control. *Stier* ordered abandoned.

12 1058hrs: *Tannenfels* recovers *Stier*'s crew.

13 1200hrs: *Stier* sinks.

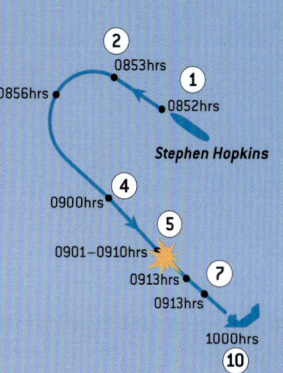

2 0853hrs
1 0852hrs
0856hrs
Stephen Hopkins
4 0900hrs
5 0901–0910hrs
0913hrs   **7**
0913hrs
1000hrs
10

N

0   1 nautical mile

0   1km

69

When *Stephen Hopkins* blundered across the mid-ocean meeting between auxiliary cruiser *Stier* and blockade runner *Tannenfels*, its master, Captain Paul Buck, refused to submit meekly. Instead, he turned his ship around. *Stier*'s captain, Kapitän zur See Horst Gerlach, ordered his ship's guns to open up on *Stephen Hopkins*, which responded with its own guns. Soon the two ships were in a furious gunnery duel. It took only a short time for *Stier*'s 15cm guns to reduce *Stephen Hopkins*. *Stier*'s light guns focused on eliminating resistance by spraying *Stephen Hopkins*'s gun crews, radio room, and pilothouse with 3.7cm and 2cm autocannon fire. In a short time, *Stephen Hopkins*'s master, helmsman, radio man, and all the gun crews were either dead or wounded. The commander of *Stephen Hopkins*'s US Navy Armed Guard proved a remarkable marksman. In less than 15 minutes he had fired the 4in stern gun 35 times, landing 15 hits on *Stier*. The hits started fires which *Stier*'s crew could not quench. Both ships were wrecks. Then a 15cm shell from *Stier* hit the 4in gun's magazine, destroying it, opening up *Stephen Hopkins*'s stern to the ocean and killing its crew. When Engine Cadet Edwin J. O'Hara reached the deck to abandon ship, he thought *Stier* was shooting at *Stephen Hopkins*'s lifeboats. To draw its fire, O'Hara manned the stern gun, single-handedly, firing the five remaining 91lb rounds that were in the ready locker before he was killed by enemy gunfire. This plate shows O'Hara firing the last round from the gun.

A cameraman aboard *Tannenfels* took this photograph of *Stier* burning before it sank. (NARA)

at his post in the engine-room station, reached the deck when the engine room was abandoned. He decided to man the 4in/50 stern gun. There were five shells remaining in the ready ammunition locker at the stern gun. He loaded and fired all five 64lb rounds at *Tannenfels*. Both German ships fired back, killing O'Hara. With that, combat ceased.

By then *Stier* was in ruins, with fires spreading uncontrollably. At 0923hrs the torpedo crew abandoned their station due to fire, which threatened the torpedo magazine. It had to be flooded. The fires grew progressively worse. Magazine 1 had to be flooded. Magazines 2 and 3 soon followed. Gerlach, trying to save his ship, ordered *Tannenfels* to prepare to tow *Stier*.

At 0955hrs Gerlach observed *Stephen Hopkins* sinking. By then conditions on *Stier* were growing worse. The engine was restarted at 1014hrs, but shut down at 1025hrs. A jury rudder was rigged, but then failed. The seas were now too rough for *Tannenfels* to come alongside to fight the fires. At 1040hrs, Gerlach ordered *Stier* abandoned. Its crew and all aboard, including several prisoners, transferred to *Tannenfels*. At around 1130hrs *Stier* sank. Two members of *Stier*'s crew were dead and 30 injured.

Stephen Hopkins managed to lower one lifeboat, with 21 men – 15 sailors and six members of the US Navy Armed Guard crew – aboard. Those aboard the lifeboat managed to evade capture by *Tannenfels*. They decided to take the lifeboat to Brazil 1,300NM west, using a sail aboard for propulsion. Two men in the lifeboat died of wounds shortly after boarding, however, and two others died during the 31-day trip. The survivors reached Brazil on October 27, 1942.

Gerlach and those aboard *Stier* reached France aboard *Tannenfels* on November 2, 1942. *Tannenfels* sailed through lead elements of the Operation *Torch* invasion fleet to reach France, and successfully delivered a cargo of rubber, metals, and medicine it had taken onboard in Japan.

STATISTICS AND ANALYSIS

The three Kriegsmarine surface raiders that broke into the Atlantic in 1942 sank 26 Allied merchant vessels and took three more as prizes, depriving the Allies of 185,700 tons of shipping. Additionally, *Michel* conducted a second cruise from Japan during which it sank three ships for 27,632 tons. The three surface raiders encountered and fought no warships, escaping from every potential encounter.

Of the ships taken, seven were US-owned (six sailing under the US flag and one using a Panamanian flag), 15 were British, five Norwegian, one Dutch, and one Greek. In total, 20 freighters, eight tankers, and a passenger liner were taken, 22 in the South Atlantic and seven in the Indian Ocean. All were sailing independently.

Most, including the vast majority of American merchantmen were new vessels. They including two Liberty ships and two Empire ships (the British equivalent of the Liberty ship) built after World War II began. Of the other five American vessels, three were US Maritime Commission designs, built since 1938; two were modern T2 tankers; and one was a new C1 freighter. The freighter *Sawokla* and tanker *William F. Humphrey* dated to 1920 and 1921, respectively.

One liner, the British-flagged SS *Menelaus*, escaped after being attacked on May 1, 1942. It outran its pursuer, *Michel*, after *Menelaus*'s engineer tied down the ship's safety valves, raising boiler pressure to three times the safe limit. It allowed *Menelaus* to make 21kn, 5kn faster than *Michel*, and was the only ship to escape the Kriegsmarine raiders after being attacked.

The types of ships taken, that they were sailing independently, and their locations when taken showed the limitations of the surface-raiding auxiliary cruisers. Operating alone,

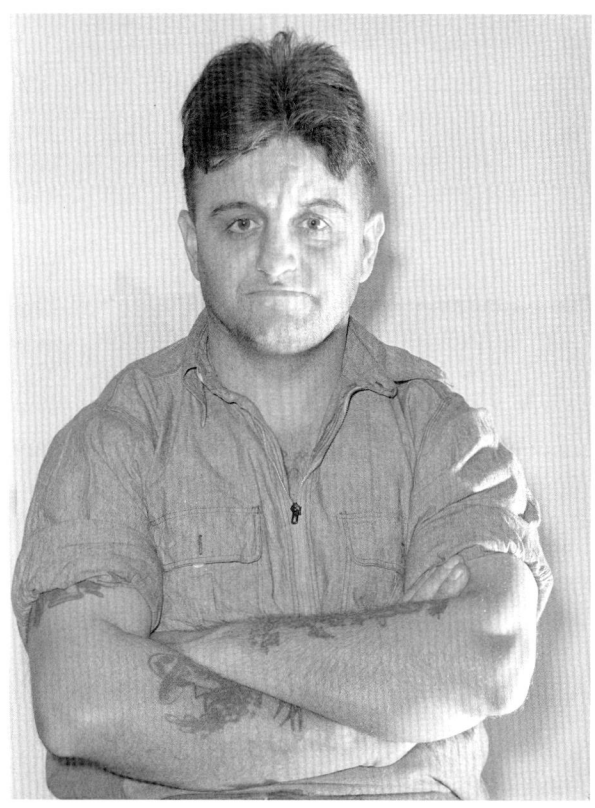

Fighting was part of the American culture in the first half of the 20th century. American sailors had a reputation for brawling more than other American working men, so it was unsurprising that many sailors were willing to fight back even against impossible odds. (Library of Congress)

with support limited to a supply ship or two, they could not take serious damage. Any damage requiring a shipyard repair would be fatal. Any protracted battle, whether with a warship or even a merchantman (as with *Stephen Hopkins*), led to destruction.

To survive auxiliary cruisers had to avoid detection by maritime patrol aircraft. Their prey was limited to individual ships, not convoys. (Since merchant vessels were armed, those in most convoys outgunned the Kriegsmarine's auxiliary cruisers, even before considering the escort.) In 1940 and 1941 those conditions could be found on much of the world's oceans. Even in the North Atlantic, through much of this period, convoys dispersed once west of Iceland or south of Cape Finisterre. Maritime patrol aircraft only covered the Eastern Atlantic and around Gibraltar, but this started changing in the last quarter of 1940.

By the end of 1941 convoys spanned the entire North Atlantic, and Allied aircraft covered the periphery of the Atlantic from Gibraltar through Canada. This eliminated most of the North Atlantic as a fruitful hunting ground for Kriegsmarine auxiliary cruisers. When the United States entered the war in 1942, only the South Atlantic and Indian Ocean remained viable. The entire Pacific was transformed into a war zone, and Allied merchant shipping fled the Far East.

Even swaths of the South Atlantic and the areas around South Africa were dangerous for auxiliary cruisers as 1942 progressed. Brazil declared war on Germany on August 22, 1942, making the western South Atlantic around that country challenging. Britain started stationing RAF Coastal Command aircraft in South Africa, and the United States built and operated an airfield on Ascension Island.

Maritime patrol aircraft constrained surface-raider operations in the northern half of the South Atlantic and within 500NM of South Africa. This forced the 1942 raiders to operate in areas with a relatively low density of shipping. The raiders sent out in 1940–41 had reasonably expected to find one opportunity to take a ship each week. The 1942 raiders were lucky to find one target per month and never more than three in one month. The difficulty in finding targets was one reason Ruckteschell of *Michel* was willing to travel 900NM to reach *George Clymer*, even though he suspected it might be a trap. He had not found another ship in the past six weeks. In another case, that of *Stephen Hopkins*, the target blundered into *Stier* in the middle of the South Atlantic Ocean. Only the fourth ship Gerlach had encountered over a six-month period, it found him.

The successful raiders, *Michel* and *Thor*, depended on the element of surprise. Seven of the 16 ships *Michel* attacked were unaware of any threat until they were attacked. In two cases, *Connecticut* and *George Clymer*, the crews did not realize their ships were being attacked by a surface raider. They thought a U-boat had launched the torpedoes striking them.

Ruckteschell made frequent use of both the torpedo boat *Esau* and darkness. Weather permitting, he lowered *Esau* into the water at the beginning of each night to serve as a scout. It found targets for *Michel*, which then made use of the darkness to approach within point-blank range before attacking. Even if a victim tried to use its guns, it was too late for an effective response. The only ship that escaped *Michel*, *Menelaus*, was attacked during the day from an initial distance of 5NM. It was the only ship attacked at that great a distance, and one of the few attacked during daylight hours.

Similarly, Kapitän zur See Günther Gumprich, commanding *Thor*, relied heavily on stealth, preferring to attack at night or during rainstorms. He made extensive use of radar, allowing *Thor* to approach a target to within 1NM before commencing his attack. The first warning a target with unwary lookouts had of *Thor*'s presence was incoming gunfire. Gumprich also made use of *Thor*'s Arado Ar 196 floatplanes to find and stalk a target. They would also take down the radio aerials of merchantmen with a grappling hook attached to a wire trailing from the aircraft. The aircraft also dropped bombs on the merchantmen.

Kapitän zur See Horst Gerlach of *Stier* was the only 1942 captain who favored conducting daylight attacks. All four of his battles took place during daylight hours, and started at distances great enough to allow the crews of the merchantmen to man their guns. In three cases, the ships fought back.

Gunfire was the most common weapon. Surface raiders fired their guns during 28 of the 30 encounters they had with merchant vessels. They fired torpedoes on seven attacks, and from *Esau* on four attacks. (Three of the four times *Esau* launched a torpedo attack, it was the only vessel attacking. On one other occasion it made a torpedo attack in combination with one by *Michel*.) On four occasions the merchantman was sunk by scuttling charges following surrender. Finally, *Thor* took three prizes.

Of the ships attacked, nine were attacked unexpectedly with little chance to resist. That included three of the seven US-flagged ships. Six ships stopped and surrendered once a warning shot was fired by the raider. Eight ships attempted to run, but only one succeeded in escaping. The other seven stopped and surrendered when it became

Increased numbers of maritime patrol aircraft and their wider global distribution as 1942 began severely restricted the free operation of Kriegsmarine surface raiders. Allied aircraft such as this Consolidated PBY-5A Catalina forced the German vessels into areas unpatrolled by aircraft and lightly traveled by merchant shipping. (US Naval History and Heritage Command)

obvious that they could not outrun their pursuer, generally not firing a shot. This included the elderly US ship *Sawokla*. Seven others, including three US-flagged ships (*Stanvac Calcutta*, *Stephen Hopkins*, and *William F. Humphrey*), shot back.

On a percentage basis, the US-owned ships were the most likely to resist given an opportunity. Three of four (75 percent) in that position resisted vigorously, while four of 11 (36 percent) British-flagged ships returned fire. None of the ships of other countries offered resistance. American crews' propensity to shoot back, even to continue firing as their ships sank under them, may have been the result of a number of causes. The US Navy provided gun crews for American ships. The United States also has a tradition of pugnacity, fighting even when faced with long, even impossible, odds. All three American merchantmen that fought back sank with guns blazing.

Only one, *Stephen Hopkins*, offered an effective resistance. *Stanvac Calcutta* achieved only two hits from 30 shots fired. *William F. Humphrey* had barely fired enough shots from its 5in/51 stern gun to register *Michel's* range when two torpedoes hit the American ship, sinking it. By contrast, *Stephen Hopkins* achieved an incredible 42 percent hit rate with its 4in/50 stern gun – something even a crack naval warship could envy. In his after-action report Gerlach stated he believed *Stephen Hopkins* to be a heavily armed "Q-ship," a disguised, heavily armed merchantman intended to trap unwary Kriegsmarine U-boats and surface raiders.

The second wave of surface raiders was less successful than the first. The first wave sank or captured 106 enemy merchant vessels, including 11 240–360-ton whale-catchers; 26 became prizes, including all the whale-catchers. This was achieved using six auxiliary cruisers. These surface raiders deprived the Allies of over 630,000 tons of shipping. By contrast, the three surface raiders of the second wave added only 29 more ships and 186,000 tons.

Increased numbers of Allied maritime patrol aircraft and ASW ships reduced the opportunities for surface raiders after 1942 ended. Ships still sailing independently were also better armed. Those at sea in 1942 were armed with whatever was available, generally World War I leftovers. As 1942 ended, new merchantmen were armed with up-to-date 5in/38 and 3in/50 guns and the highly effective 20mm Oerlikon. These weapons gave newer merchantmen a great deal more firepower than the 4in/50 and 3in/23 guns carried by *Stanvac Calcutta* and *Stephen Hopkins*.

AFTERMATH

The third wave of raiders petered out completely, the three ships unable to break into the Atlantic. *Komet* was sunk traveling down the Channel trying to force its way into the Atlantic. *Togo* (tentatively renamed *Coronel*) was forced back. Since it failed to arrive at the Biscay coast, it retained its original name, serving as a minesweeper and again as a night-fighter-direction ship. *Hansa* was converted, but by the time it was ready to sail in 1944, the French Atlantic ports were unavailable. Instead of being a hunter, it spent the rest of the war as a target, a practice ship for training U-boat crews.

The auxiliary cruiser faded away because the Kriegsmarine found a more effective commerce raider: the U-boat. An auxiliary cruiser had a crew of 300–400 men. A Type IX U-boat had a crew of 48–56. The Type IXC U-boat had a range over 13,000NM, and the Type IXD 23,700NM. The most successful auxiliary cruiser took 146,000 tons of enemy shipping. The top-scoring U-boat sank 306,000 tons and 14 other U-boats scored over 150,000 tons, all while using one-eighth the crew of an auxiliary cruiser. However romantic the auxiliary cruiser appeared, it proved an increasingly ineffective tool as the war continued.

Of the ten ships converted to auxiliary cruisers by the Kriegsmarine, only *Widder*, *Togo*, and *Hansa* survived the war. *Widder* was converted to a repair ship upon returning to Germany in 1940, and renamed *Neumark*. After the war, it was given to the British as a war prize, becoming the freighter *Ulysses*. Sold back to Germany in 1951, it was renamed *Fechenheim*; on October 3, 1955, it beached off Bergen, Norway, and broke up over the next six days. *Hansa* was returned to the Glen Line at war's end and served under its original name, *Glengarry*. It remained in service with the company through at least 1967. It was later sold and eventually scrapped in 1971.

Togo lasted longest. A war prize, it was transferred to Britain at war's end, the United States in January 1946, and the Norwegian Navy in March 1946 as *Svalbard*. Used mainly as a transport, the Norwegians sold it in 1954. In November 1956, its original owners repurchased it, restoring its original name. They sold it in 1968. After a number of further ownership and name changes, it was finally wrecked in 1984.

The American merchantmen the auxiliary cruisers hunted proved more resilient, one reason being there were a lot more of them than of their hunters. The US Maritime Commission built massive numbers of merchantmen between 1937 and 1945 – nearly 6,000 including 2,708 Liberty ships. Only 200 Liberty ships were lost to all causes during World War II, including structural failure. The 2,551 survivors filled the world's merchant fleets over the next quarter-century, along with the over 2,500 other US Maritime Commission-designed ships built during that period.

While many aged out, the advent of the container ship made every World War II-era freighter economically obsolete. It was cheaper to build and operate new container ships than convert existing break-bulk ships. Most of the surviving World War II-era freighters went to breakers' yards in the 1960s and 1970s, but several large C4 freighters and troopships were converted to container ships. Those lasted longer, into the 1980s or 1990s, but they were the first ships sent to the breakers' yards at the sign of any economic downturn. It was cheaper to scrap them than hold onto them.

Today only seven World War II-era cargo ships still exist – four Liberty ships (SS *Albert M. Boe* (renamed *Star of Kodiak*), SS *Arthur M. Huddell* (renamed *Hellas Liberty*), SS *Jeremiah O'Brien*, and SS *John W. Brown*) and three of the VC2 Victory ships that replaced them. All are museum ships, six in the United States and one in Greece.

FURTHER READING

There is surprisingly little about the surface raider war in official histories. The most comprehensive coverage of the second-wave German raiders in those sources is largely in Roskill's history of the Royal Navy in World War II. Morison has fragments so minor I left him out of my bibliography. This is unsurprising when one considers the peripheral nature of the surface raiders to the Allies. The only country that would feature them in official histories was Nazi Germany, the total destruction of which ensured no official histories were written by the regime.

Instead, I pieced together the story from sources specifically about the campaign or individual battles within the surface-raider war. Some are overenthusiastic and have to be approached with care. Others, like Schmallenbach's *German Raiders*, are excellent. I supplemented my research with online sites and with Norman Friedman's works, especially as related to weaponry. Some online sources are listed below. I think I was able to put together an accurate portrayal of an obscure part of World War II naval history.

http://www.navweaps.com/
https://www.wrecksite.eu/
http://uboat.net

Friedman, Norman (2013). *Naval Anti-Aircraft Guns and Gunnery*. Annapolis, MD: Naval Institute Press. First published in 1981.

Lane, Frederic C. (2001). *Ships for Victory: A History of Shipbuilding under the U. S. Maritime Commission in World War II*. Baltimore, MD: Johns Hopkins University Press.

Muggenthaler, August Karl (1977). *German Raiders of World War II: The first complete history of Germany's ocean marauders – the last of a great era of naval warfare*. Englewood Cliffs, NJ: Prentiss-Hall.

Reminick, Gerald (2006). *Action in the South Atlantic: The Sinking of the German Raider* Stier *by the Liberty Ship* Stephen Hopkins. Palo Alto, CA: The Glencannon Press.

Roskill, S.W. (1956). *History of the Second World War, War at Sea, 1939–45: The Period of Balance Vol. 2*. London: Her Majesty's Stationary Office.

Sawyer, L.A. & W.H. Mitchell (1985). *The Liberty Ships: The History of the 'Emergency' type Caro ships constructed in the United States during the Second World War*. Second Edition. Colchester: Lloyds of London Press.

Schmallenbach, Paul (1979). *German Raiders: A History of Auxiliary Cruisers of the German Navy, 1895–1945*. Cambridge: Patrick Stephens.

INDEX

References to illustrations are shown in **bold**.